THE **WI** A CENTURY IN THE MAKING

MAVIS CURTIS

AMBERLEY

To Ellie and Catherine, two feminists of the future.

First published 2015
This edition published 2016

Amberley Publishing
The Hill, Stroud
Gloucestershire, GL5 4EP

www.amberley-books.com

Copyright © Mavis Curtis, 2015, 2016

The right of Mavis Curtis to be identified as
the Author of this work has been asserted in
accordance with the Copyrights, Designs and
Patents Act 1988.

ISBN 978 1 4456 5540 6 (paperback)
ISBN 978 1 4456 1704 6 (ebook)

British Library Cataloguing in Publication Data.
A catalogue record for this book is available
from the British Library.

Typesetting and Origination by Amberley
Publishing
Printed in the UK.

Social insurance fully developed may provide income security. It is an attack on Want. But Want is only one of five giants on the road to reconstruction and in some ways the easiest to attack. The others are Disease, Ignorance, Squalor, and Idleness.

Sir William Beveridge, The Beveridge Report, 1942

CONTENTS

INTRODUCTION

In 1942 when Sir William Beveridge put before Parliament his report, unsurprisingly called the Beveridge Report, he identified, in remarkably poetic language, the five giants Britain needed to fight. They were Want, Disease, Ignorance, Squalor and Idleness. In that one sentence he identified what the Women's Institute had been fighting against since 1915, when the first branches of the movement were formed.

Not that I knew anything at all about five giants or indeed the WI. Brought up in the industrial West Riding, I'd never heard of the WI. There was no branch in our working-class suburb of Huddersfield and there was a good reason for this. The WI for most of its life was a countrywoman's organisation. Women in towns had the Townswomen's Guild, at least they did after 1928, when the WI helped to set it up.

It was only on moving to rural Oxfordshire that I came to hear and read about the WI, and that was because I began to research the history of the village I had moved to, Elsfield, well known, at least in Oxfordshire, as the home in the 1920s and 1930s of John Buchan, author of historical biographies but now mainly known as the creator of novels such as *Greenmantle* and *The Thirty-Nine Steps*.

John Buchan's wife Susan founded the Elsfield branch of the WI in 1919 when the Buchan family moved to the village. It was reading the minutes of that organisation that opened my eyes to the revolutionary effects the movement must have had on this village, and therefore, one can assume, on villages like it throughout the length and breadth of the country. Susan Buchan writes about her arrival in the country in the aftermath of the First World War: 'The dwellers in Elsfield were completely turned in on themselves. The Women's Institute did bring something into the village which helped to take minds off the endless gossip about the daily life of neighbours.'

It is not always easy to discover what women have achieved. A prime example is Dr Rosalie Jobson. Look her up on Wikipedia and the only way she can be found is because she married Gordon Morgan Holmes. There's a lot about him. He was a neurologist, and appointed to the British Expeditionary Force in France during the First World War. Later knighted, he proposed to Rosalie Jobson while they were rowing on the Thames. She was an Oxford graduate and an international sportswoman. And that's as much as we know from that source. But she was also one of seven members of the Women's Hospital Corps, who were turned down by the War Office when they offered their services for work in France during the First World War but went anyway, funded by the Women's Suffrage movement.

Why did no-one record what these women did? Because in the nineteenth and well into the twentieth century, women's influence was often exercised through the men in their lives. Men of note find their way into the National Dictionary of Biography and thence into Wikipedia. It is not always, or even often, that has happened for women. For one thing, women change their names on marriage and for another, history, until fairly recently, has been written by men about men – political rather than social history. It was a system run by men who just did not see what the women were contributing to society. With women excluded from the political process until a hundred years ago in England, there was nothing men felt needed to be said about women. There were, of course, exceptions such as Florence Nightingale, but Mary Seacole, who worked in a similar context, was a black woman and therefore doubly invisible, and she has only become noticed relatively recently when women and black people's contribution to history has been acknowledged.

Women's groups have also had a similarly low profile so to know what women did and what they thought, one often has to look at who they met, people they were in touch with, and the networks they were part of. Virginia Woolf, for instance, is well known for her writing and being part of the Bloomsbury group, but the information that is not so readily available about her is that she was also a supporter of the Co-operative Women' Guild and treasurer of her local branch of the WI. She was also a friend of Susan Buchan, to whom she wrote her last letter before committing suicide.

In the latter half of the nineteenth century and early part of the twentieth, there was a flow of women from one organisation to another, as there is today. Today, if someone is interested in, say, the environment, they may well belong to Greenpeace, Friends of the Earth and the Green Party and they will know people with similar interests. So it was at the beginning of the twentieth century, when liberal-leaning women might well find themselves involved with the suffrage movement, women's education or the welfare of unmarried mothers. I have therefore spent some time looking at the background influences in the lives of Trudie Denman and Grace Hadow, two of the most important founder members of the WI, so we can see just why they arrived at their way of thinking and the actions that sprang from their philosophy.

From its inception in 1915 until the 1950s and 1960s, the WI became a significant place for both the working-class women of the village and their middle-class counterparts. For working-class women, the WI provided a place where they could enjoy a leisure activity, while for middle-class women, who were largely the ones who ran the branches, it was an outlet for their organisational skills. Nothing shows this more clearly than E. M. Delafield's *Diary of a Provincial Lady*, a fictionalised account of a middle-class woman's life in the West Country in the 1930s. Her daughter had a governess, her son was away at school. All she had to do was organise the cook and the housemaid, who tended to gang up on her. How on earth was she to fill her time? Well, she joined the WI, which provided her with meetings to organise, talks to prepare and people to supervise.

As Maggie Andrews has pointed out in her book *The Acceptable Face of Feminism*, the WI was the largest women's organisation in the post-suffrage era, one of its distinctive features being that it was exclusively for women. There were men involved in the WI in its early days between 1915 and 1918, but when the WI formed a national federation independent of government they were made honorary members without any executive power. Maggie Andrews also claims that the WI is a feminist organisation, a claim which many WI people would contest. But if we accept her definition of a feminist organisation, 'any group of women who challenge the boundaries of feminine behaviour, whether in economic, political or cultural terms', if we include women who struggle to gain improvements in the lives of women, then the WI must be termed 'feminist', as its history shows.

A women-only organisation can be both supportive and empowering for women, and conversely disempowering for men. The local WI created a space where women could explore their own interests and abilities away from the censure of the men in their lives. Old Mont in *Lifting the Latch*, a moving and honest account of country life in the first half of the twentieth century, refers to the WI as a 'new-fangled revolutionary' organisation. Mont says at one point, 'One of the first things our Mam were taught by that dangerous Women's Institute were to make a simple hat of natural straw, plaited round and down from a pointed crown with ribbons to tie under the chin.' Now, Mont may have called the WI revolutionary and dangerous with a twinkle in his eye, especially as the revolution resulted in nothing more than a plaited straw hat. Hardly the stuff of revolution, one might think. But in terms of what had been available for village women in the past, and what it signified to both the men and women of the village, it was indeed revolutionary. Here were women who had skills and whose skills were worth fostering.

One aspect of this revolutionary approach was the significant role the WI played in renegotiating domesticity. The WI view of women was concerned with domesticity, but not passive domesticity. The WI valued the work women did in the home, even though it was unpaid. Their definition of domesticity was more politically aware. Women's work was perceived as skilled, skills could be improved, and since their work had value, the women themselves felt they were entitled to some leisure time. The WI provided an alternative value system to that of the men of the village, a system which not only valued women's skills but provided training to improve them.

With its emphasis on domestic skills, attendance at a WI meeting could be seen as an acceptable leisure pursuit. So the monthly WI meeting could be justified on two counts: firstly, they were entitled to some time off their (unpaid) work at home, and secondly, they were increasing the skills they already had by attending demonstrations and talks about such matters as dress-making or home nursing. And the importance of a healthy home environment and knowledge of household management had been acknowledged by the Prime Minister Lloyd George himself in 1918 when he had promised better housing – Homes fit for Heroes. This attitude to domesticity stood the WI in good stead until the rise of the new wave of feminists in the 1970s, who felt that women should emancipate themselves from domesticity, if they so wished, and engage with the world of work outside the home.

The WI became such an important part of country life that any book set in the country, if it had any claims to authenticity, assumed that the fictional women of the village all belonged to the WI. So we see Agatha Christie writing in *The Moving Finger* that the envelopes containing poison-pen letters were all typed on the WI typewriter, and Ngaio Marsh started *Grave Mistake* with the WI meeting. More recent writing uses the WI as shorthand for respectability and common sense. So Victoria Wood shows a hysterical young woman being brought back to normality by a brisk slap to the face and the admonition, 'This is the WI. If you want to panic, join the Townswomen's Guild.'

These fictionalised accounts are verified by a non-fiction account of how the WI came to play such an important part in the lives of middle-class women, written by Miss Phyllis Wickham, who lived in Sutton Scotney in Hampshire. Her autobiography, hand written, tells us how she was recruited and the part she played as a Voluntary County Officer (VCO) in supporting the branches during the twenties, thirties and forties. She begins her account by placing herself socially. 'The daughter of a doctor and the granddaughter of a Winchester College schoolmaster, I am one of the women who, as a spinster, lived at home and was untrained in any career.' Leaving school in 1917, she was one of the women who did not marry because of the dearth of suitable young men in the aftermath of the First World War.

Another account of life as a middle-class woman and supporter of the WI, this time in the Midlands, is contained in the war diaries of Mrs Milburn. She wrote, though not for publication, while the bombs dropped on Coventry and she sheltered in the dugout in her garden, and she shows how the middle-class women of the country provided a social network which held village society together.

This is a history of the WI in England and Wales. Unfortunately there is not space to cover the story of Scotland or Northern Ireland. Scotland has its own organisation, the Scottish Women's Rural Institute, known to its members as 'The Rural'. It is one of the largest organisations for women in Scotland and its aims are to advance the education and training of those who live in the country, and to promote the preservation and development of Scotland's traditions, rural heritage and culture. Like the English and Welsh organisations, it traces its roots to Adelaide Hoodless and Stoney Creek, began life in 1917 and has a magazine still called *Home and Country*. The Northern Ireland Women's Institute began life rather later, in 1932. It is, of course, a small federation, but there is plenty going on there, nevertheless. There is a music festival, a drama festival, a golf competition, they had a presence at the eightieth anniversary celebration of Stormont, and there is also a three-day event at Balmoral Hall (the Irish Balmoral, not the Scottish), which is their chief fundraising event.

Society has changed a great deal in the course of the last hundred years. The WI has sometimes brought these changes about, sometimes adapted to them and sometimes failed to change as rapidly as society demanded. I have tried to put the WI into the political context of its time, to show how, to begin with, it was often at the forefront of thinking on social issues and how effective it was at the tasks it set itself. The story of the WI could be seen as the rise, fall, and rise again of the organisation. The federation in the 1920s and 1930s knew what it wanted and where it was going. After the Second World War and the establishment of the Welfare State, much of what the institute had worked for had come about. I have tried to show the difficulties they encountered in their struggle to adapt to this change of circumstances. I have examined whether or not they were successful in this, and how in the end the WI was given relevance to more modern times by the actions of its grass-roots members.

Set up in a time of war by a government put in power before women were enfranchised, with the aim of increasing food production for the country and rejuvenating village life, the WI's role in the life of the country was expanded by the women who had been staunch supporters of the suffrage movement. They turned the institution into a vehicle for educating women, not just in household skills, but in their role as fully enfranchised citizens.

In the *Guardian* of 4 June 2013 there was an article marking the centenary of the death of Emily Wilding Davison, the suffragette who was killed by the king's horse at Epsom. In it, several prominent members of our society were asked if they thought there was more progress to be made on women's rights. As you can imagine, they all said there was much to be done to make society fairer for women. Among these was the well-known comedian Jo Brand, who appears to be a well-informed woman on many topics. This is what she said:

> We need to take domestic violence much more seriously, address the trafficking of women, and improve women's knowledge when it comes to safety. But underlying all this is an attitude problem: there isn't enough respect for women. You can see that in all sorts of ways – an obvious one is the treatment of older women on TV, with those who do appear being criticised for their looks, and others being pushed off screen as if all they're good for is the WI and scone-making.

If a well-informed and intelligent woman can sideline the WI in this way, it seems important to ask why she has arrived at this conclusion. Why does an organisation with such a powerful history of fighting to improve living and working conditions for women seem irrelevant to women such as Ms Brand? Perhaps we may have a better idea by the end of the book.

In her book *The Women of the Cousins' War*, the well-known historian Philippa Gregory has said that in writing history, 'selection is inevitable. These days we understand that only a partial story can ever be told ... There is no such thing as unbiased unprejudiced history.' I hope the story I tell here has not been so deliberately selected that it gives an inaccurate picture of the WI, though I dare say it is a partial story. There are other narratives that could be told, but here is the story as I see it.

I

WADDLING SWANS ON BOWLING GREENS: THE POSITION OF WOMEN IN THE NINETEENTH AND BEGINNING OF THE TWENTIETH CENTURIES

The National Federation of Women's Institutes was formed in 1918, though the true beginning of individual Women's Institutes was rather earlier, in 1915. This was of course when the First World War was in its second year and was lasting rather longer than expected. But the establishment of the WI was not just the beginning of an organisation, it was the culmination of a gradual improvement to women's position in society in the nineteenth century and could not have happened without the clear thinking, the constant lobbying, the political nagging, and in the end the violence that some women were prepared to perpetrate to improve their position in society.

As we learned at school, much of the nineteenth century was taken up with the Industrial Revolution, when throngs of people left the land to earn a living from the new industries in towns and cities. We can see the changes in society in the censuses, which took place every ten years from 1841. In 1851, 50 per cent of the population of England and Wales were classified as urban dwellers, a figure which had increased to 75 per cent by 1891. During the course of the nineteenth century, London's population increased from a million plus in 1809 to almost 2 million in 1850, and by 1891 had reached 4 million.

Agriculture did very well in the twenty years from about 1850 to 1870 because of the demand for food from the urban population, food which could be easily and quickly transported on the newly built railways. However, as the Americas, Australia and New Zealand began exporting their produce to the British Isles – grain from the prairies of America and refrigerated meat from the Antipodes and Argentina – the market for British produce plummeted. Villages were no longer the lively and prosperous places they had been.

During the course of the nineteenth century, therefore, living conditions for many people, whether in the town or the country, were squalid and unhealthy, in the towns because the growth in decent housing and sanitation could not keep pace with the increasing population, and in villages because of the sheer poverty brought about by stagnation in the rural economy. Indeed, by the beginning of the twentieth century the poor physical condition of the men turned down as recruits for the Boer War led to the setting up of a Government Committee on Physical Degeneration. This concluded that mothers needed educating about nutrition so that the next generation of soldiers would be considerably better than the present poor physical specimens. What they didn't seem to realise is that poverty might have had something to do with it, and that access to nutritious food was restricted because families couldn't afford it.

There was also 'The Woman Question'. The Victorians had rather painted themselves into a corner where women were concerned. Many people had rigid views about what was appropriate behaviour for the different sexes. Ideally middle- and upper-class women, people who aspired to be 'ladies' or had already attained that status either through birth or hard work were considered to be physically weak, as indeed they may well have been, since their access to exercise and fresh air were in many cases restricted. Eleanor Lodge, in adult life principal of Westfield College, spoke of her days with a Mrs Lovell, who took in young ladies to educate them. 'We certainly sat in rooms with all the windows shut till we felt faint; and if the wind was in the east she did not even let us out. ... My legs used to ache with longing to run hard and go far, but it was very seldom that we seemed to get any distance or to be out for more than three-quarters of an hour.' It has to be said, however, that Eleanor Lodge may have been exceptional. She was a great walker and cycler when she escaped from Mrs Lovell's care, thinking nothing of cycling or walking forty miles in a day. She was also extraordinarily thin. Her brother Oliver, an Oxford don, records that at one time she was five foot eight inches tall and weighed only five stone eight pounds. She never tired either physically or mentally, and eventually she was sent to a German spa 'to try to get up strength and a more wholesome feeling of fatigue'.

Perhaps, being so very thin, Eleanor Lodge had no need of corsets, but the majority of women did. These were sometimes laced so tightly that women's internal organs could be displaced, with the stomach and liver pushed down towards the abdomen, causing digestive difficulties. Their lungs were restricted so they found breathing difficult and expanding their lungs impossible. They also began wearing long dresses at the age of seventeen, when they came out into society, and these prevented unladylike running about. A stately progress was what ladies aimed for. When tennis became fashionable in the 1870s, *Sylvia's Home Journal* noted that there was some truth in a critic's comment that 'women taking an active part in a lawn-tennis competition may be compared to a swan waddling on a bowling green, for women clad in the dresses of the present day were never intended by Providence to run'.

There was an ongoing discussion about the role of men and women in nineteenth-century Britain. Ideally, a woman was pure, spiritual and morally strong. A woman's place was in the home, looking after husband, household and children, which should fulfil all her needs. Tennyson expressed the ideal in his poem 'The Princess':

> Man for the Field and Woman for the Hearth
> Man for the Sword and for the Needle she.
> Man with the Head and Woman with the Heart.
> Man to command and Woman to obey.
> All else confusion.

But what about those women who had no husband or children? For them there were good works. It was quite acceptable for ladies to extend their nurturing to the poor of the parish or fallen women, and most ladies did so, providing of course that they had someone to chaperone them wherever they went. Even in the 1880s the American-born Duchess of Marlborough was surprised to find that it was not considered the done thing for a lady to walk in Piccadilly or Bond Street without a chaperone.

Ladies were often channelled into good works through their church, and through a genuine desire to improve others' lives and perhaps also to justify their own privileged existence. There were good causes in abundance to support.

There were plenty of non-political groups women could join. Within the Church of England the Mothers' Union was begun in 1876 and the Girls' Friendly Society in 1876, and there were managerial roles open to women – they could stand as Poor Law Guardians, and, after the 1870 Education Act, for school boards. The NSPCC was founded in 1884, one of the many voluntary societies which absorbed middle-class women's energies. Some became prison visitors, others taught the children of the poor while one young woman, Sarah Robinson, a brave soul indeed, tried to reclaim women from a brothel in Aldershot. In her book *Life as a Victorian Lady*, Pamela Brown describes how Sarah paced up and down outside the building, praying for strength, before dashing inside. 'I could not write down, I cannot even bear to think of the horrible things I saw and heard', she wrote. She was violently sick when she got home, but persisted, nevertheless and is reputed to have saved five to ten girls a week, while her two companions prayed and sang outside the brothel to give her courage. Other women turned their attention to health matters, working for such organisations as the Red Cross, formed in Britain in 1870.

For middle-class women, paid work outside the home, except as a governess, could not even be thought of, except for such bohemian characters as the Brontë sisters or Mary Jane Evans (George Eliot), who had to publish their books under male pseudonyms.

Philanthropy gave middle- and upper-class women a role in life, and at the same time infantilised the poor. Presumably the poor preferred to be patronised rather than starve, but they paid by their gratitude and deference for the puddings and clothing supplied by the upper classes, a system supported and justified by the Church.

'All things bright and beautiful', with its memorable and now rarely sung words, expresses the Victorian attitude to perfection.

> The rich man in his castle, the poor man at this gate
> God made them high and lowly, He gave them their estate.

There were differing attitudes to the philanthropic work undertaken by women. Wilkie Collins in *The Moonstone* makes fun of spinster ladies who carry leaflets with them at all times with a view to 'helping' or converting others less fortunate than themselves. Miss Clack, who is a member of the Select Committee of the Mothers'-Small-Clothes-Conversion-Society, which rescues unredeemed trousers from the pawnbroker and cuts them down to fit their young sons, has tried unsuccessfully to give a tract to the maid who lets her in at her rich relations' house. 'She handed me back the tract and opened the door. We must sow the good seed somehow. I waited till the door was shut on me, and slipped the tract into the letter box.'

This was written in the mid-nineteenth century, and opinions had changed somewhat by the end of the century. In 1893, the International Exhibition, held in Chicago and dedicated to showing what people had achieved in the course of the century, featured for the first time a section on work undertaken by women. The exhibition included a published report entitled *Woman's Mission* in which the organiser, Baroness Angela Burdett-Coutts, wrote, 'It is fitting that the close of the nineteenth century should focus and illustrate in a definite form the share which women have taken in its development, of which, in my humble judgement, the truest and noblest, because the most natural, part is to be found in philanthropic work.'

Of course, some women, working-class women, such as the maid who opened the door to Miss Clack, had to work to keep middle-class households functioning. In the Victorian era the number of families who could afford to employ servants rose steeply. The greater the number of servants you employed, the greater your standing in society. By 1901 being a servant was the major source of employment for women. With a total workforce of one and a half million it was the largest source of employment in the country.

The position of women in prosperous households when Victoria came to the throne in 1837 was an unenviable one. They did not have the vote and were excluded from many kinds of direct political involvement. They were, for instance, excluded from the discussion about the slave trade at an anti-slave trade conference in 1840, which did not go down well with the women who had been actively involved in the anti-slavery movement. On marriage a woman's money went directly to her husband, so she had no independent source of income. Nor did she have control of her children in the event of a separation. In the first half of the century one woman, Caroline Norton, had left her husband because he was alcoholic and abusive, but she had no access to her children and was prevented by him from visiting one of her children, who was dying. This drove her to work to limit the control husbands had over their wives. In the Custody of Infants Act 1839 children were declared not to be the property of their father in certain cases and in 1858 the Matrimonial Causes Act was enacted, which allowed a woman who left her husband to retain anything she had inherited or owned after they had separated. Finally, in 1882, the Married Women's Property Act ensured that married women could retain independent ownership of their own property. This did not apply to the poor, who had little or nothing, so it was largely useful to middle- and upper-class women.

As the century progressed women gradually chipped away at these restraints and injustices. In the political field, though they did not have a vote, women managed to influence political thought through indirect lobbying and support for the two political parties, the Liberals and the Conservatives. In 1881 the Fabian Society, open to both men and women, was set up to discuss socialism, and two years later the Conservative Party established their own support group, the Primrose League. Set up originally for the men of the party, it soon acquired a women's branch, founded in 1885. Realising they might be missing a trick here, the Liberals also established a similar group with its Women's Federation, started in 1886, which took up the cause of women's suffrage.

Working women in mills and factories campaigned for improvements to working and living conditions. By the 1880s the Women's Co-operative Guild was formed, the Women's Trade Union Association in 1889, and the Women's Industrial Council in 1894, all striving for improvements in women's working conditions. But collective lobbying for improvements in working conditions was difficult for servants, who as individuals were scattered, unlike mill and factory workers.

There was also an interest in providing better education for girls and young women, which was, as one might expect, a very strong movement in Oxford. There was resentment among many middle-class women because they were denied access to university education, which was deemed a right for their brothers. Middle-class girls were often educated at home, or sent to boarding schools, where the educational standards were abysmal. The living conditions at these schools also left much to be desired. Eleanor Lodge, for instance, describes the food at the school she attended in Wolverhampton: for breakfast they had two slices of bread and scrape (very thinly spread butter, margarine or dripping), the bread was 'like chaff; it was specially stale as being better for us' and was also, of course, cheaper than fresh bread. 'At eleven in the morning a plate of dry bread was handed round and cold water was available.' They did, however, have a substantial dinner of meat and a pudding. Tea, she says, was a repetition of breakfast, with an occasional treat of bread and treacle, and supper was another two slices of bread. Enough to keep children from starving, but precious little in the way of protein or fruit, which would be deemed essential in a modern diet.

Middle-class women such as Eleanor Lodge, though they often had a disrupted and fragmented education, also often had brothers who moved on from school to university in Oxford, Cambridge or London. Eleanor herself was the youngest of nine children, the only girl, and when her brother Richard, then a fellow at Brasenose College, suggested she should follow him to Oxford, she obtained a place at Lady Margaret Hall under the wing of the principal, Elizabeth Wordsworth. From being a student there she evolved into a tutor. This was not a paid post, but she could charge pupils for the tutorials she gave them.

In the early nineteenth century women were not admitted to the University of Oxford, but in the 1870s pressure from the wives of academics (who had recently been allowed to marry) made academic lectures available to women, eventually leading to the creation of the Association for the Education of Women (AEW), founded in 1870. This led directly to the foundation of two colleges for women, Somerville, named after the astronomer Mary Somerville, and Lady Margaret Hall, named after Margaret Beaufort, mother of Henry VII.

The colleges only concerned themselves with housing students and lectures were arranged by the AEW on an individual basis. At first lectures were given by fellows of the men's colleges exclusively to the women, but eventually the ladies were allowed to attend lectures in the men's colleges, accompanied at all times by chaperones. Somerville Hall could only accommodate seven of the twelve students who had been enrolled. The five others, and thirty other students living at home or with friends, became known as Oxford Home Students, which very much later in the 1950s became St Anne's College. The home students became the direct responsibility of the secretary of the AEW. Their movements in the city were severely limited; they had to be accompanied everywhere by a chaperone. When the bicycle was first introduced it was considered scandalous for women to use this mode of transport.

These women, often the children of clergymen, discovered that education had given them a purpose other than the domestic duties that had formerly been their only way forward. As Vera Brittain has pointed out, they were learning to 'use their faculties; to recognise and define their aims; to develop a respect for accurate knowledge ... and to endure failure and disappointment, if it came, with the consciousness that part of a pioneer's equipment was the refusal to accept defeat'.

It was a turbulent time and it is not surprising to see that by the end of the century Lionel Woolf, husband of Virginia, could write of his university years, 1897 to 1902, 'We found ourselves living in the springtime of a conscious revolt against the social, political, religious, moral, intellectual and artistic institutions, beliefs and standards of our fathers.' And mothers, he might have added if he had been writing even twenty years later.

The Suffrage Movement

Amid all this political ferment, one of the most well-remembered, and ultimately successful, movements was that for women's suffrage, formed in 1872. We probably all know about the suffragettes – the Pankhursts, and Emily Wilding Davison, who studied at St Hugh's, Oxford University, and was later killed by the king's horse at the Derby.

What is less well known is that after the success of the suffrage campaign some of these women went on to set up and run the Women's Institute. Such a one was Edith Rigby, who planted a bomb in the Liverpool Corn Exchange and burned down Lord Leverhulme's wooden house on Rivington Pike. She founded a club for girls working in the weaving sheds of the local mills and took them out to the park to play cricket in their clogs. She, like many other militant suffragettes, went on hunger strike and was force-fed in prison. Married to a long-suffering doctor, Edith refused to confine her servants to the attics and basements of their house: the maids ate in the dining room, wore no uniforms and had the evenings off. The evening the cook went to the theatre, leaving Dr Rigby a meal of sandwiches, proved something of a flash point with his wife. When he complained she left the house. Dr Rigby waited patiently for her to return, as it was not the first time this had happened. When she had not returned after a couple of weeks he hired detectives to trace her. She was working as an under housemaid in a large house in London. When he asked how she could treat him in this way, she replied, 'I'm sorry, sir, we're not allowed followers.' She did, however, return to him.

In 1912, the Liberal Prime Minister Asquith, who had promised the vote to women, put a stop to the Conciliation Bill, which would have given women the vote, a move which alienated many women who had supported the Liberal Party. Many of them transferred their allegiance to the newly formed Labour Party, and Edith reacted in typically violent fashion. She poured acid on the green of the local golf course and suggested to a friend that she should plant a bomb in the mouth of a cannon in a Blackburn park. As the friend had time on her hands before returning to Preston, where they both lived, she set fire to the stands at Blackburn Rovers Football Club. When the battle for votes for women had been won, Edith transferred her energies to the WI and founded the Hutton and Howick branch of the WI.

The WI was the natural extension of the suffrage movement. Many of the leading lights of the organisation had been active workers for women's right to vote, including the first national chairman, Lady Denman, through her involvement with the Liberal Party, and her deputy, Grace Hadow, through the Oxford-based suffrage society. The first treasurer of the institution was Mrs Auerbach, who had been treasurer of the National Union of Women's Suffrage Societies (NUWSS) working alongside the political activist Millicent Fawcett. Lady Isabel Margesson, a member of the Women's Social and Political Union (WSPU), was on the committee, and Inez Ferguson, the first general secretary of the WI, had been secretary of the National Union of Societies for Equal Citizenship (NUSEC). Unsurprisingly, these women were keen to see the WI encourage its members to become politically aware.

Most of the women who founded and ran the WI, at both national and local level, were suffragists, rather than suffragettes, and deplored the use of force, though it was acknowledged by Grace Hadow, the first vice-president of the WI, that violence had triumphed where many years of patient demonstrations and lobbying had not. These women were often supporters of the Liberal Party, and after the First World War, when the vote was granted to women over the age of thirty, they turned their attention to how best to promote the welfare of women in this new and exciting world where women could play an active part in the political world as well as the world of good works and the home. Many of them, including Edith Rigby, turned to the newly formed Women's Institutes as a way of informing, educating and supporting women in their new role.

Grace Hadow, who was to become the first vice-president and was recognised as the most intellectual of the founding members, had been a member of the Women Students' Suffrage Society (WSSS) founded in 1907. She took part in the great procession to the Albert Hall in 1908 behind a splendid banner, and became president of the Oxford Women Students' Society for Women's Suffrage (OWSSWS) from its formation in 1911 until 1915. From its inception, key members of the executive committee and organisers of OWSSWS spoke at numerous open-air and drawing-room gatherings. The group was organised by a subcommittee of local sympathisers, and speakers included Miss Hadow. The secretary from 1914 to 1915 was Helena Deneke, a great friend of Grace Hadow, who was to become a very enthusiastic and stalwart member of the organisation and a longstanding member of Elsfield WI.

Both Helena Deneke and Eleanor Lodge went on the pilgrimage organised in 1913 by the National Union of Women's Suffrage Societies. This had several strands to it. People set off from several places in England to converge at London for a great rally. Not everyone walked the whole way, but people joined in and took part in stretches of the journey. The branch which passed through Oxford set off from Cumbria. The aims of the rally were two-fold: to show how many women supported the suffrage movement, and to demonstrate that women could organise a big event such as this. It was estimated that 50,000 women arrived in Hyde Park at the end of the pilgrimage. The banner which the Oxford women marched behind was used later in the coronation procession and in the culmination of the pilgrimage.

The greatest political success of the early WI was Margaret Wintringham, who, on the death of her husband, the MP for Louth, stood for Parliament and was voted in in 1921 at the by-election caused by his death. In Parliament she worked alongside Nancy Astor to retain the employment of women police officers in peacetime. The year after becoming an MP she was voted on to the executive of the NFWI. She said that her years of membership of the WI were the best training she could have had for her work as an MP. While Margaret Wintringham may have been the most politically successful woman to take advantage of the newfound political freedom, there were triumphs at a local level, jubilantly recorded in the WI magazine *Home and Country*. Mrs Shepherd of Battle WI stood for her local council and was elected, while Mrs Wood of Lewes St Anne's branch was elected to the council as its first woman councillor.

The link between the suffrage movement and the WI was acknowledged by the general public. The anthem inextricably linked to the WI, 'Jerusalem', the words of which were written by William Blake in 1816, was set to music by Parry in 1916 and was originally written for a concert on behalf of the 'Fight for Right' ultra-patriotic movement. Parry became unhappy with this movement and finally withdrew his support. The song was taken up by the Women's Suffrage movement and Millicent Fawcett, president of the NUWSS, asked if it could be used at a Suffrage Demonstration Concert on 13 March 1918. Parry was very pleased. After the concert Millicent Fawcett asked if it could become the Women Voters' Hymn. Parry was delighted, and assigned the copyright to the NUWSS. When the NUWSS was wound up in 1928, Parry's executors reassigned the copyright to the WI. The National Federation of Women's Institutes (NFWI) adopted the colours of the suffragist movement – the green, violet and white of the Women's Social and Political Union. The colours are significant. They stand for G (give) V (votes) for W (women).

The WI was exclusively rural, but when women in the towns wanted to form institutes, the National Federation decided that they should focus particularly on the needs of women in the rural communities and with the support of the NFWI, the Townswomen's Guild was formed in 1928.

The WI saw itself as a body which could and should educate its members to take an active role in local and national politics. As one speaker put it at the 1919 AGM, 'Now that we have this educating body, let us educate our people to realise that it is their duty as citizens to take their part in Parish and District Councils.'

2

FRUITFUL, NOT FRIVOLOUS: THE BEGINNINGS OF THE WOMEN'S INSTITUTE

In spite of the plethora of movements to improve life in town and city, the impetus for the foundation of the Women's Institute came not from England but from Canada, and from one woman in particular who, like Caroline Norton, was motivated by personal tragedy to work towards a better-informed society. Her name was Adelaide Hoodless, whose fourth child, John Harold, had died aged fourteen months of something called 'summer complaint', caught from drinking contaminated milk. She believed that if she and the farmer's wife who supplied the milk had known more about how to look after milk in hot weather, her son might not have died, and she spent the rest of her life working for domestic science lessons, both in schools and with women who had left school but who needed to improve their household knowledge.

Adelaide was one of a group of women who founded the Hamilton branch of the Young Women's Christian Association (YWCA) to provide education for working-class unskilled women, many of whom were young immigrant workers, isolated from their mothers who would traditionally have taught them home management, and at sea in a country whose climate was different from their country of origin. The YWCA was initially a place for them to stay, but Adelaide Hoodless soon introduced typing lessons and domestic science. The title 'domestic science' was a way of accrediting a scientific basis to women's work and thus putting it on a par with men's. From this base in 1896 Adelaide persuaded the National Council of Women to back her campaign for the introduction of domestic science into the school curriculum. From there it was a small step to extending that knowledge to women who had already left school, but who needed more mental stimulation and practical knowledge of running a home or farm.

What she had to say was heard by Erland Lee, secretary of the Farmers' Institute of Wentworth County, who promptly booked her the following year, 1897, for the next ladies' night of the institute in Stoney Creek. Thirty-five women were present for a talk on the importance of domestic science for girls. Why not, they wondered, form a sister organisation to the Farmers' Union where people could learn from speakers and from their neighbours? All the women present expressed an interest, so Erland Lee and his wife Janet spent the next week advertising the idea.

A week later they organised a meeting, which was attended by 101 women. They aimed to promote the knowledge of household science, sanitation, a better understanding of the value of different kinds of food and a more scientific approach to childcare, so that the health of the next generation would be improved. Mrs Hoodless remained in contact as honorary president of Stoney Creek Women's Institute, and it was her suggestion in 1902 that the WI motto 'Home and Country' should be adopted.

From this vigorous beginning the movement spread rapidly. In 1900, the Ontario government, realising its worth in terms of education in food production and the improved mental health of rural women because it broke down their social isolation, began to give ten dollars as a start-up grant to new groups. Adelaide Hoodless, along with Lady Aberdeen, the Governor-General's wife, also set up the Victoria Order of Nurses to reach families in remote settlements. Lady Aberdeen returned to England in 1898 and the following year Adelaide Hoodless followed her, to spread the word about the Canadian Women's Institutes and how they were educating women, breaking down their isolation and loneliness and generally improving life for everyone. The best thing since sliced bread, they might have said, if sliced bread had been around. Adelaide died in harness, on the platform of a Women's Institute meeting in 1910.

Lady Aberdeen was a member of an English organisation which called itself the Women's Institute, though it had very little in common with the Canadian version. For one thing, it was a city organisation, and had been set up by a keen suffragist, Mrs Nora Wynford Phillips, in 1897. Its aims were very different and rather grander than the Canadian model. Its goal was to provide a meeting place and centre of information for the convenience of women who were engaged in all departments of public and professional work. More like a men's club, really, with talks on a variety of subjects – eugenics, government bills affecting women, female education, and so on. This Women's Institute linked itself to other organisations such as the National Council of Women, founded by Mrs Louisa Creighton (wife of the Bishop of London and a founder member of the AEW, which, we have seen, was working for access to university-level education for women), and the Rural Educational Union, founded by Lady Warwick (the 'Daisy' of music hall fame).

As a young and not so young woman, Lady Warwick had embarked on a series of affairs with various important men, including the Prince of Wales, later King Edward VII. She had one great failing as a courtesan: she was so indiscreet she was known as 'the babbling brook'! When she became rather long in the tooth for the role of courtesan, she turned her attention to rural affairs and philanthropy, founding a hostel for students of agriculture at Reading College, which later became the University of Reading. In 1915, along with Lady Aberdeen, she organised a display of 'what women have done and can do in agriculture', which was held in the garden of a resplendent house in Carlton Terrace belonging to Lord and Lady Cowdrey and co-hosted by Lady Cowdrey and her daughter Trudie, Lady Denman.

Meanwhile, two years earlier in 1913, another personal tragedy precipitated the arrival in Britain of yet another forceful Canadian woman, Madge Watt. She was a graduate of Toronto University and widow of Dr Alfred Tennyson Watt, who had recently been accused of professional misconduct and had thrown himself from the balcony of the hospital ward where he was being treated for depression. With the double blow of professional disgrace and suicide to deal with, Madge fled Canada with her two boys and arrived in Britain ostensibly to provide a better education for her sons. In British Columbia Madge had been a founder member of the first Women's Institute there, and had soon become a WI lecturer and organiser. The Canadian movement was very closely linked to the government, and in 1911 this became a formal link when an advisory board of four women was appointed to the Department of Agriculture of British Columbia.

In England, with her boys newly settled at boarding school, Madge set about promoting the growth of Women's Institutes following the Canadian model. She thought it would be an aim easily attained, since there was already an awareness of the need to encourage self-help and co-operation in the farming community, embodied in the Agricultural Organisation Society (AOS), a government-funded body that aimed to restore some prosperity to the farming industry. The secretary of the AOS, John Nugent Harris, had already tried to do something similar to what had been done in Canada, so he had invited wives and daughters of the farmers who attended AOS meetings to come along. His idea was greeted with indifference and suspicion. Countrywomen knew their place and had no intention of stepping out of it. Certainly not at the bidding of a man, an official from London at that. Their own communities were often less than enthusiastic about any initiative that would enhance the lives of women. In one village the vicar had forbidden the women to venture out after dark, and another village thought taking a woman away from the kitchen sink was a dangerous thing to do. Who knew where it might lead? Nugent Harris became quite frustrated and said that even if they came to the meeting the women refused to talk. They 'sat silent and took no part in discussions. They sat there like oysters,' he fumed. 'After the meeting they would come up and criticise what had gone on,' he continued. When asked why they wouldn't join in the discussions, they replied, 'We dare not because our husbands and sons would make fun of us.'

Madge Watt tried the same approach as Nugent Harris with as little success. She had brought with her from Canada an introduction to Nugent Harris but didn't bother using it. She tackled matters head on and went to as many women's meetings as she could find, especially if they had an agricultural element. However, the English class system meant that nothing could happen in a village without the approval of the squire and his lady, and the Church saw no need for a new women's group since there was the Mothers' Union, so Madge Watt had no success.

After two years of fruitless labour, in 1915, with the country now at war, Madge Watt had got to the point of giving up. As a last resort, she spoke at an Agricultural and Horticultural Union meeting and was heard by Nugent Harris, who was so excited at what she had to say that he booked her immediately as a speaker at the AGM of the AOS, whose work was becoming increasingly urgent as the country sought to increase agricultural production to make itself independent of imported food. Madge Watt sat at the front of the auditorium with her knitting and listened to speaker after speaker. When it was her turn, she put down her knitting and told the assembly of her work establishing Women's Institutes in Canada. There followed a resolution proposing that the Canadian model of Women's Co-operative Institutes should be adapted to English rural life, and this should be done with the government being responsible for the work. The resolution was put at the end of the meeting when the hall was beginning to empty, and Robertson Scott, the radical journalist who was still in the hall and who later went on to found the magazine *The Countryman*, was of the opinion that many who voted were unsure what they were voting for! Since the idea of co-operation was important, the first suggestion for a name for the new organisation was the Women's Co-operative Institute, but this was rather too near to the Women's Co-operative Guild to be acceptable, so the name settled on was the Women's Institute, in spite of there being an organisation with the same name, which seemed to have been moribund by this time.

By now, of course, the men of the country were being leached away from their communities to fight in Belgium, many of them never to return, and women were being forced willy-nilly into thinking for themselves and doing jobs that until now had been the preserve of their menfolk.

One of Nugent Harris' staunchest supporters was the chairman of the North Wales branch of the AOS, Colonel the Hon. Richard Stapleton-Cotton. Colonel Stapleton-Cotton, a relative of the Marquess of Anglesey, had returned to Anglesey after having been struck by lightning on his sugar plantation in Antigua. The lightning strike had resulted in his legs being paralysed from the knee down, and he travelled round the countryside in a large bath chair pulled by a donkey. When the war started he encouraged the local women to work on his land. He set up an egg-collecting depot at the station and travelled round the farms in the area collecting and marketing the eggs for them. The cracked and broken ones were sold off cheap. He also grew flower bulbs, which went off on the train along with the eggs. He ran a chicory farm and owned a bacon factory, so he was a very important local employer.

The colonel promptly asked Madge Watt to go down to Anglesey to speak to his village, Llanfair PG. Would she go? Of course she would! She talked to the people at the meeting he called, who promptly formed a branch of the WI on the spot. The colonel's wife was made president of the branch and a committee was chosen. Madge made it clear that the institute should rule itself with four freedoms to be kept as cornerstones of the organisation: Truth, Tolerance, Justice and Friendship. The institute would therefore cut across all the barriers that local village society had been divided by: class, creed (particularly important in Wales, where church and chapel never met) and political allegiance. 'Make it fun, otherwise you won't attract the young ones,' said Madge, 'but fruitful not frivolous.' The aims of the organisation were five-fold: to study home economics, to provide a centre for educational and social activities, to encourage home and local industries, to develop co-operative industries and to stimulate interest in the agricultural industry.

Subscriptions were fixed at two shillings a year, at a time when agricultural wages were thirty shillings a week. All elections were to be by secret ballot and a clear procedure for the running of the meeting was laid out as follows:

1. Opening
2. Minutes
3. Correspondence
4. Roll Call
5. Reports
6. New business
7. Reception of new members
8. Programme and discussion
9. Adjournment.

Their first meeting place was somewhat problematic. They couldn't use church or chapel facilities because that would tie it to one particular religious group, so Colonel Stapleton finally settled on a damp and ivy-covered garden room – a large shed, really – in the garden of the Marquess of Anglesey's surveyor, and this is where the very first branch of the Women's Institute was established.

With Madge Watt employed by the AOS on a temporary basis with the specific remit of founding branches of the Women's Institute, and with the social cachet of a close relative of a marquess and marchioness having set up a successful branch, the movement took off. Generally it was someone in the upper echelons of the village hierarchy who became president of the branch, but committees were elected according to one member, one vote, and the vote was secret. This was considerably too radical and democratic for some people and led to opposition in some quarters, for example, the lady who expected to be elected president of her branch and was not, and consequently signalled her disapproval of the decision by nailing up her front door, and the wife of the vicar, who was similarly disappointed when the presence of her husband at the inaugural meeting had no effect on the ballot and who then fixed the church council meeting at the same time as the WI with only one item on the agenda – 'the Suppression of the WI'! By October 1917, however, there were 187 branches with a membership of just over 5,000, and county federations were forming to provide support for newly emerging branches.

The form of the monthly meetings was set very early on in the organisation's life. The meeting was held either in the afternoon or the evening and lasted two or three hours. It began with 'business', i.e. the organisation of the institute, county and national WI issues, which was followed by a talk or demonstration.

It was soon realised that with the growth of branches and the spontaneous formation of county federations a national federation was needed to co-ordinate all these individual bursts of activity. The government refused to give the AOS any money to run a national federation, though the Board of Agriculture's food production department did agree to fund the formation of new institutes and to subsidise the new county federations. Lady Denman (Gertrude to her family and Trudles to her father Lord Cowdrey), who was elected chairman of this new national organisation, was adamant that it could not function well if it were funded by the government as it would be seen as just another government department. The National Federation of Women's Institutes had to be self-funding. A deputy to Lady Denman was soon appointed, Grace Hadow, a blue-stocking from Oxford who had already set up several WI branches in Gloucestershire, where she was born. Lady Denman and Grace Hadow worked together for twenty years to put the WI on the map and steer it through the choppy waters of the 1920s and 1930s, until Grace Hadow's death in 1940.

The emergent WI was a natural place for suffragists, and even suffragettes, to find a home. It was non-denominational, non-party-political, and also largely pacifist. It drew its support from the rural community and because of its origins it retained the thread of interest in food production and rural crafts, which had been perceived to be on the decline, while expanding the educational horizons of its members to prepare them for their new role as full citizens of the state. One of the great achievements of these early English and Welsh WIs was that they harnessed the tradition of 'do-gooding', which the middle and upper classes had established in the nineteenth century, but gave it a more democratic twist by including the working classes as equals. (This was in theory. In fact everyone in village society knew their place and knew the appropriate behaviour for that social position.)

Gertrude Denman, the first chairman of the organisation, a role which she would hold for the next twenty five years, was elected yearly in a secret ballot. Her biographer, Gervas Huxley, considers that the personal qualities she brought to the job were courage, truth and absolute fairness and honesty. She also had a sense of balance and proportion, and she had an objective outlook, regarding everything in an impersonal, disinterested way. That makes her sound rather cold and distant, but she was very kind to individuals and had a great sense of fun, so no meeting was ever dull.

The first AGM of the Women's Institutes was held on 16 October 1917, at a time when the submarine blockade by the Germans had made Britain a beleaguered island with only a few weeks' food supply left. In 1919, county federations which had grown up in a number of places were brought into the national structure, and the National Federation of Women's Institutes (NFWI) devised a set of rules they were invited to adopt. Representatives of the counties also formed a consultative council, which met twice a year to oversee internal affairs of the NFWI and wider political issues that affected rural women. In the same year the federation established a magazine, *Home and Country*, the title copied from their Canadian counterpart. The title is an interesting one. The word 'home' carries with it all kinds of emotional connotations. As Maggie Andrews has pointed out in her analysis of the WI, the rural home had been epitomised in the First World War as an image of England that soldiers were fighting for, and many postcards from the front carried somewhat idealised pictures of rural cottages.

To many people, home has always represented safety and order. As Jeanette Winterson has pointed out, 'Home is much more than shelter; home is the centre of gravity ... When we move house, we take with us the invisible concept of home.' For her, 'Home was problematic. It did not represent order and it did not represent safety.' Immediately following the First World War, returning home meant coming back to a loving place for the men who had suffered unimaginable hardships and horrors. It was natural, then, that women should see themselves as the heart of the nation and the home as the centre of their kingdom. It was no surprise, therefore, that the focus of much of WI thinking was the domestic scene.

Over 500 delegates attended the second annual meeting of the NFWI in 1918, where the aims of the organisation were spelled out:

The Women's Institute Movement was started to provide means for the effective development of the part countrywomen can play in rural development by supplying an organisation in country districts through which an educational policy can be given full effect, and by which the knowledge gained can be applied practically in the different branches of agriculture, rural industries, domestic science, hygiene and social welfare.

From the outset Lady Denman was determined that the movement should be financially independent as soon as possible. Being from a family used to business, she decided that there should be a reserve capital and promised that if the organisation could contribute £5,000 she would match it. The treasurer of the NFWI, Mrs Auerbach, set about raising the money in 1920 and by the end of the year had succeeded in raising £6,600. Due to the treasurer's good management the movement became completely financially independent by 1927, the year Mrs Auerbach retired from her post.

A number of Voluntary County Organisers (VCOs) were appointed by the county organisations to help with recruitment. They had a uniform and hat which were available from Harrods, there was a training school for them, and expenses of three pounds a month were paid, once they had been trained. The VCOs were initially from the upper classes, since they had the physical means to do the job – the use of a car, servants to do the work at home and the confidence. They in turn recruited willing middle-class members who they felt would be suitable for the job. Miss Phyllis Wickham of Sutton Scotney was one such lady. She lived in a village that had a lively social life. There was the hockey club, the badminton club, the Shakespeare reading club, and, particularly at Christmas time, dances, parties and entertainments. Sutton Scotney WI was founded in 1917, its first president being Mrs Courage, who lived at Sutton Manor. Their first meeting in the village hall was lit by oil lamps and heated by a coal fire. Miss Wickham herself lived with her mother in a thatched rented cottage with few amenities.

In the 1920s Miss Wickham first came to the attention of the chairman of the Hampshire Federation, Mrs Bostock, because of her links with the Wolf Cubs (the old name for Cub Scouts). She occasionally adapted the games she learned as a Wolf Cub leader for her local WI, and one such game, which she calls a 'mime burlesque', was so successful that it made her something of a celebrity in the local WI community. Mrs Bostock, the VCO for Hampshire, was the wife of Sam Bostock, who had been secretary of the AOS and had worked with Madge Watt and Nugent Harris.

Mrs Courage took Miss Wickham along to county federation meetings as a 'general dogsbody and secretary', and when Mrs Courage retired from her job as VCO, Miss Wickham was asked to put her name forward as a replacement. She writes,

> I've no way of knowing what misgivings they had at letting loose
> a young spinster living in a thatched cottage but, on looking back,

one realises that it was a bit of a breakaway from the 'feudal system' and they must have known it would be the beginning of a more representative cross-section of the membership taking responsibility for leading the Institute.

It was certainly that. As a demonstration of the democratisation of the organisation, Miss Wickham cites a training session for all the Hampshire VCOs that necessitated an overnight stay. Mrs Bostock had the responsibility of looking after another VCO, Lady Wells, helping her dress for dinner and seeing she got to bed safely, because it was the first time Lady Wells had travelled without her personal maid.

Mrs Bostock encouraged Miss Wickham to take part at the county level, which became much easier to do when she acquired a car, an Austin 7 Tourer, which was 'a bit draughty and hard of seat'. In this Miss Wickham travelled up to London for the 1929 AGM. 'Before this,' she writes, 'we had not had much contact with the WI outside our own village.' There was plenty of parking behind the Albert Hall. 'I shall never forget my first experience of that huge meeting and the realisation that there were so many other WI members in England and Wales.'

For her VCO training, Miss Wickham travelled up to London then out to Broxbourne in Essex, where she was initiated into the secrets of being a successful VCO by Mrs Nugent Harris and a Miss Hurst Simpson, who had cropped hair, masculine coats and shirts with collar and tie, and was interested in horticulture and agriculture.

Miss Wickham became involved in the home industries which WI members were encouraged to set up. She lists rush work, gloves and linen embroidery as small businesses that could sell their wares at the WI shop in Winchester on a commission basis. 'Members were very keen and if you were accepted as a worker attaining a good standard you received a very nice little addition to your pocket money', she says. Sutton Scotney had its own speciality – hand-made underwear. 'We were immersed in pink crepe de chine; lovely plain needlework, faggot stitching and embroidery,' Miss Wickham comments.

Miss Wickham devised her first talk on 'comradeship' in 1934, which Mrs Bostock helped to put together. The VCO's job, as well as giving talks, was to start new branches, suspend any branch which was in difficulties, and be a link between branches and county federation. One of her responsibilities, she remembers, was to pass on information about vitamins and to encourage a scientific approach to nutrition. Later she 'got up' a talk on wild flowers, their folk lore and their herbal value, illustrated by large placards she had painted herself. One was used as a Christmas card by Dorset County Federation when she moved there after the war to keep house for her brother following the death of her mother.

Miss Wickham is remarkably outspoken about her personal circumstances. As well as documenting her and her mother's pleasure at having running water and electricity installed in their cottage, she also records having lunch with Miss Chamberlain, sister of Prime Minister Neville Chamberlain, who had taken on the chairmanship of the Hampshire County Federation following the retirement of Mrs Bostock. This was soon after she had had all her teeth extracted and was the nervous possessor of a full set of false teeth. She wondered how she would manage. 'I had butterflies in my stomach because the anticipation of coping with anything but mince was a real anxiety.' She managed roast lamb with 'fair success'.

As we can see from Miss Wickham's account of how she became a VCO, there was little democracy about the organisation at that stage. Much depended on who you knew and were known by. This continued for many years, as we shall see in the account of Betty Christmas' involvement at Denman College. It certainly provided a network of countrywomen who could work together for what they saw as the good of the country in general and women in particular, but it made for a conservative organisation, which over the century developed a tendency to look inward rather than out to the wider community.

A great deal of power over the direction the WI should take resided with the national executive – the people at the top exercised their influence over their subordinates. The rules of the National Federation were adopted by a conference of representatives of the first 137 Women's Institutes at Central Hall, Westminster, in October 1917. It was followed in 1918 by the first AGM, which under the guidance of Grace Hadow became the first policy-making meeting of the organisation. Any resolution with a two-thirds majority on a public question was put before the relevant government minister. All institutes had equal voting rights and as many members as possible were encouraged to attend, assisted by a system of pooling the costs of travel among every branch, so those who had to travel farthest were not disadvantaged. There is more about the national constitution in Chapter 4.

3

'A SPLENDID SHOW IN THE WINDOW': LADY DENMAN

As we have seen, the first chairman of the WI, Lady Denman, retained the post from 1917 until 1948, being voted in unanimously every year. Lady Denman, an energetic and formidable woman of decisive views, was born in 1884, the second of the four children of Weetman Pearson, soon to be made Lord Cowdrey, and his wife Annie Cass. She was christened Gertrude Mary, but was known to the family as Trudie, or by her father as Trudles. She was very close to her father, a Yorkshire man whose family business was engineering. With all the engineering projects so beloved of the Victorians, there was a great deal of work for S. Pearson & Son, and aged twenty-eight, Weetman, as head of the company, moved to London to set up the firm's headquarters there. There was no engineering project the Pearson empire could not tackle. They built dams, they dug tunnels, they built munitions factories. Weetman made an awful lot of money. He was a staunch Liberal in politics, a believer in free trade, Home Rule for Ireland and women's suffrage, old-age pensions and sickness insurance. When he turned his attention to politics he was elected MP for Colchester, a position he held for fifteen years. While away from home on business, he nevertheless saw it as his job to provide guidance to his daughter, and often wrote to her. In one letter he said,

> Dame Fortune is very elusive. The only way to succeed with her is to sketch a fortune which you think you can realise and then go for it bald-headed. The headaches, the fears, the ceaseless work (which starts each morning as if nature had not been exhausted the night before, but existed in inexhaustible generosity), the endless disappointments that will be met not only each day but many times a day, the sacrifices that have to be made, all become incidents that have to be overcome and forgotten.

Trudie was in no doubt, then, that success had to be worked for and did not come easily. Weetman was a good employer who valued the work put in by his men. He took a personal interest in the people who worked for him and labour difficulties were largely unknown in his company. His wife Annie was a partner in her husband's enterprises, accompanying him to Mexico and sleeping rough, exposed to all weathers, if need be. She was never afraid of responsibility. They were a formidable pair. There was a close bond between Weetman and his daughter 'Trudles'. He was devoted to her, and her admiration for him was intense. According to her biographer, Gervas Huxley, of all his children she was probably the most like him in character and outlook. Her father may have been absent for much of her young life but he maintained a presence in his letters. One he sent her in 1903, which she kept, answered her letter describing how she had only earned twopence from going carol singing with a group of friends. Her father wrote, 'That twopence ought to be treasured as now you will know what earning money means. There are many twopences that every successful man (or woman) whatever their careers may be, has to work as hard for as you did for yours.' He goes on to advise her that

> the only true course to follow is remain as near the commonplace and average as your surroundings will allow you. But at the same time it is necessary to have large reserves, so that at any time you can push your way to the front should it be necessary ... This line of conduct brings respect and love and will 'get you there at the finish'. Hence be careful to avoid having nothing behind. If you can make a splendid show in the window, do so, so long as there will be no disappointment when the interior of the shop is examined.

Late Victorian society, with its strict rules of etiquette and restricting views of what constituted suitable behaviour for women, did not suit Trudie Pearson. She had a dreary education at home with a succession of governesses, one of whom had a pet monkey, which Trudie was supposed to look after. She then attended a small private school before being sent to Dresden to be 'finished'. Her mother, Annie, who worked for the improvement of nursing and helped found the College of Nursing and the Cowdrey Club for members of the nursing profession, had a curious mixture of liberal and conservative views and actions. She rode a bicycle, which was rather daring at the time, but made sure it was a silver one from Tiffany's, so everyone would know she had money. She was a keen suffragist, though when it came to her daughter's future she took the old-fashioned view that you married a 'suitable' young man, one who would help the family climb higher up the slippery social pole, a feat which money alone could not achieve. A good husband should be someone rather higher up the social scale, someone with good breeding. So Trudie, when her time came to marry, was strongly encouraged to accept Thomas Denman, a young army officer of good family with an exemplary record of service in the Boer War, but whom she barely knew and didn't find in the least attractive. Annie was not above a bit of emotional blackmail and when Trudie refused him, Annie developed a nervous illness which cleared up immediately when Trudie reluctantly agreed to marry Thomas. The wedding dress was fully illustrated in the fashion papers and her going away hat, which had a stuffed brown owl with glass eyes as decoration, was much admired. The wedding was reported in one newspaper as having 'a soupçon of New York about it' and the groom was reported to have a streaming cold and to look very ill.

It would be nice to think that Trudie found happiness with Thomas Denman, but what happiness she did find had little to do with her husband, and there must have been precious little happiness for him, married to a wife with so much energy and so little respect for convention. Thomas Denman was looking for a wife who would act as a prop to him, who would help him further his career and take good care of his health, which was precarious. Thomas suffered from hay fever in the summer, which meant he took long cruises. Trudie was a poor sailor. He suffered from bronchitis and asthma in the winter, while Trudie smoked like a chimney. Nevertheless they had two children, Thomas, born in 1905 and Judith, born 1907. Trudie wrote that during her pregnancy with the latter she had tried to cut down on her cigarette smoking, and had managed to smoke only three a day.

Her father gave her a mansion, Balcombe Place, in West Sussex, with its accompanying 3,000 acres, so there were some compensations. Trudie could ride round her estate, organising the cutting of timber and improving the cottages – installing sanitation and running water, conveniences which did not arrive in some parts of England until the 1950s. She loved riding to hounds and fox-hunting.

At her mother's suggestion, in 1908 she joined the executive committee of the Women's Liberal Federation, which was working towards electoral reform by peaceful means. This organisation was presided over by Lady Carlisle, a formidable woman with such a zeal for temperance that she was reputed (inaccurately) to have poured the contents of the wine cellar at Castle Howard, the family seat, down the drain. With Lady Carlisle as leader, the group formed an influential political body and pressure group. The main concern of this group in the early years of the century was women's suffrage, though the members were very opposed to the violent measures used by the suffragettes under Mrs Pankhurst.

When Trudie joined the Women's Liberal Federation executive the Liberal Prime Minister of the time, Asquith, had just promised that an Electoral Reform Bill would be introduced that would extend the male franchise and would not oppose an amendment giving the vote to women, provided that the demand for women's suffrage had the overwhelming support of the country's women. With the increase in violence by the militant suffragettes, public opinion was draining away from their cause, and this affected the Liberal Party. In the run up to the 1909 election, when Lloyd George tried to introduce social reforms which would redistribute wealth and establish an old-age pensions scheme and health insurance, the Women's Liberal Federation formed area federations, and Trudie was made chairman of the Metropolitan branch, a signal tribute to her powers of organisation. The new scheme in London proved highly satisfactory, a reflection of Trudie's good sense, energy and hard work. Her father's daughter, indeed.

Trudie learned a great deal during her involvement with this liberal organisation. She watched how Lady Carlisle worked – intervening here, sending a letter there, pulling strings and leaning on cabinet ministers if need be. She learned how to handle people with strongly divergent views and put aside her own innate shyness. Here she developed an understanding of the importance of procedure and of the mechanics of public service, which were to stand her in good stead when she became involved with the WI.

This involvement in liberal politics came to an end in 1910, when her husband was made Governor-General of Australia at the very young age of thirty-six. Trudie found being the Governor-General's wife very constricting. 'I am so grand that I am not allowed to go to any but epoch making functions of a national character,' she wrote to her brother Geoffrey. There was a prodigious amount of official entertaining, which Trudie hated. 'We spend money like water,' she wrote, 'and everything is frightfully expensive, except mutton.' And the work was so repetitive. 'Same old review of cadets, gave the same old garden party, went round the same old hospitals and met the same old people, at least they all seem the same people.' When they had to visit Tasmania there was a slight difference. When they attended a service in the cathedral they were met at the door and accompanied down the aisle by the clergy. 'It was as embarrassing as getting married again,' she commented.

The tedium of being a grand lady was relieved occasionally, however, by a day at the races or hunting each week, and if the weather was wet she played hockey in the ballroom or, a newly acquired skill, golf along the corridors, dotting cushions here and there to represent bunkers. 'We broke one globe and one glass door and gave a State picture a very nasty jar,' she wrote home. She could also escape incognito, sometimes into the bush, where rather than ride side-saddle she could practice her newly acquired skill of riding astride, and go camping, which she loved. Of the hunting she wrote to her brother, 'You have to gallop like mad over rough scrub full of rabbit holes. You had better not mention hunting to mother,' she added judiciously.

She wanted to improve life for other women. Her predecessor, Lady Dudley, had instigated the Bush Nursing Scheme, which trained women for medical work in the outback, modelled on Canada's Victoria Nurses, and Trudie was shocked to find that though the scheme had been instigated in 1909, only one nurse had been appointed. Trudie set to work and organised meetings, fundraising and generally focussing attention on the organisation so that by the time she left Australia in 1913 there were twenty nursing centres in the state of Victoria. Trudie visited some of these centres herself and shocked some of the local people by wearing riding breeches and smoking a cigarette.

Through her work with the Bush Nursing Scheme, Trudie became involved with the National Council of Women. Women already had the vote in Australia and each state was keen to encourage good citizenship among the members of the National Council. Trudie suggested that representatives of each state council should meet nationally, and she addressed their gathering in Sydney in 1912. The home of the Governor-General was in Melbourne, there being no national capital as yet, and here Trudie became very involved with raising money for the Repertory Theatre Club and the Arts and Crafts Club. She teamed up with Dame Nellie Melba, and between them they raised on one occasion alone £1,000 by organising an exhibition of antiques, which 20,000 people paid to see.

The capital of the country was established and finally finished in 1913, and it was Trudie who named the new city. Up to the moment when she opened the envelope containing the name, no-one had been sure how to pronounce it. Trudie put the stress on the first syllable – CANberra – and so it has remained. Soon afterwards she returned to England, leaving Thomas behind. The official explanation was that she was exhausted from all the work she had undertaken, though for a woman of her undoubted energy that seems doubtful. The suggestion that it may have been to distance herself – or be distanced – from a romantic liaison with a member of the diplomatic staff seems more likely. She returned to Australia later the same year, but her husband's health was suffering and the couple returned permanently to England in May 1914. The then Prime Minister of Australia, Joseph Cook, thought Lord Denman the best Governor-General Australia had ever had, and Trudie was told she was 'the last woman Australia would willingly part with'.

On their return to England on the brink of war, Thomas joined the Middlesex Yeomanry while his wife threw herself into charitable work. Unsurprisingly she joined the Smokes for Wounded Soldiers and Sailors Society, which supplied tobacco to military hospitals and to ports where the wounded were repatriated, and she soon became its chairman. The ballroom at their home in Buckingham Gate became the packing station, where presumably Trudie could smoke to her heart's content. The voluntary workers met all hospital ships and trains and supplied all the service hospitals with free smokes. Trudie became the chairman in 1916, and when she resigned due to pressure of work in 1917 nearly £67,000 had been raised, which paid for 265 million cigarettes as well as large quantities of tobacco, pipes and cigars.

At this point she suggested to her husband that as they were neither of them happy, perhaps they should separate, but Lord Denman pleaded against a permanent separation. Trudie's youngest brother, Geoffrey, had been killed in the early months of the war. These unhappy events were relieved to some extent by the arrival of her good friend Nellie Grant, who returned from Kenya when her husband joined the forces.

Trudie, though a prodigal spender when need be, was determined in these difficult times not to waste food, so she established chicken coops in her back garden at Buckingham Gate. Not content just to keep chickens, she and Nellie commissioned a friend to design a model henhouse suitable for anyone with a back yard. They advertised and managed to persuade friends and hospitals to install chicken coops, and as a consequence were inundated with requests for information and advice. She became president of the women's section of the Poultry Association, and in October 1916, following the display of what women could do at her mother's splendid house in Carlton Crescent, she was asked to join the Agricultural Organisation Society (AOS), an offshoot of the Ministry of Agriculture founded to encourage self-help and co-operation in the farming community.

A new women's branch of the Board of Agriculture and Fisheries had been set up, its aim being to form a Women's Land Army, to provide a mobile force of workers who would go anywhere to supplement the local workforce. The subcommittee, of which Trudie was chairman, was transferred to this. Trudie's friend Nellie Grant, who had had to leave England to follow her husband to Spain, now joined Trudie and was appointed organiser of the Land Army in Dorset and later Winchester.

She and Trudie travelled the country rallying people to the

cause. They would drive into a town centre and summon people to hear what they had to say with the use of a policeman's alarm rattle. Standing on the running board of their car, one of them would make an impassioned plea to the assembled throng to join the war effort in the fields of England. They sometimes spoke in theatres or cinemas, and once followed an act of performing dogs. They had a riotous reception on one occasion from an audience of sailors, and at Southampton they joined a parade of Women's Royal Naval Service (WRNS) and Women's Auxiliary Army Corps (WAAC), both founded in 1917. As they would have had to walk seven miles in the procession, they hired horses and were the only mounted people in the parade.

When they were up to their usual tricks one day in Guildford, Nellie Grant was astonished to be dragged by Trudie into a shop doorway. When she asked why, Trudie gestured to a large yellow Rolls Royce sweeping by driven by the Pearsons' chauffeur with Lady Cowdrey, Trudie's mother, in the back. Trudie thought it better for her mother not to know what she was doing as she would have couched her disapproval in no uncertain terms.

By this time, October 1917, 137 branches of the WI had already been established, watched over by the women's section of the AOS, under the auspices of Dame Meriel Talbot, known as Slasher Talbot because of her skills at cricket. Trudie Denman saw the WI as a force for social reform, and intended to make sure that aim was at the forefront of the movement. 'I was convinced that country women were overlooked by the authorities and that unless they got together to put their case this unhappy state of things would continue,' she said. It became her mission to change this position. 'How was I to convince a Government department that if these village societies were to be controlled by a Ministry or by local Authorities their value would be nil?' In the event she had no need to persuade anyone. 'Slasher' Talbot was in hearty agreement with her. A Women's Institute section was formed in Miss Talbot's branch of the Board of Agriculture, and Trudie Denman was appointed honorary assistant director to take charge of the new section. Madge Watt was appointed organiser, with three full-time salaried assistants, and the WI was on its way.

Trudie Denman was, like her father before her, a hard worker. Not only was she involved with the WI, but her family connections involved her in the administration of the Westminster Press, an organisation which controlled sixteen regional newspapers. She concerned herself with the working conditions of the women employees, in particular the provision of a pension fund. She proposed that the directors should take a cut in fees to extend the pension fund so it included all the women employees. She and her sister-in-law, non-salaried directors, were the first to reduce their income from the organisation, at which point the other directors followed suit. She also inherited her mother's interests in the Cowdrey Trust and was an executive member of the Land Settlement Association. This association, set up in 1934, resettled unemployed labourers from the North and Wales and gave them five acres of land and a newly built cottage to rent. They were expected to work co-operatively as smallholders, selling their produce communally. The organisation survived until 1983, when it was wound up and the houses sold off to their tenants. Lady Denman was also a trustee of the Carnegie Trust UK, and president of the Ladies' Golf Union, a role she held from 1932 to 1938. She also took a lively interest in the affairs of Balcombe village where she lived. She herself designed and had built both a new block of cottages on her estate and the Balcombe Victory

Hall, a community centre for the village to be managed by the Men's Club and the Women's Institute.

Perhaps the bravest work she undertook was to help found the National Birth Control Council. She had given money to Marie Stopes, founder of several birth control clinics, who had been the butt of outraged public opinion, but by the late 1920s public opinion was much more supportive of the idea of family planning, so in 1930 Trudie accepted the chairmanship of the new council. Trudie had long felt that the medical advice that was available to the wealthy should be accessible to women who were not well off to prevent them being worn out by pregnancies which they had no control over. She was determined to help them. She knew she would need fortitude to work with such an organisation when there was still a great deal of prejudice against the ideas it put forward, but she was determined to take an active part.

The first thing she did was to give the organisation the use of two rooms in a house she owned in Ecclestone Street, and the second was to appoint a woman who had applied for the job of administrator for the WI and had not been chosen – Mrs Margaret Pyke – who soon became one of her closest friends and remained so for the rest of her life. Because of the extreme caution of the government in establishing birth control clinics, the council decided to encourage the provision of voluntary clinics. By 1933 the British Medical Council felt able to lend its premises to the council for a conference attended by 125 medical officers of health. In 1940 the organisation changed its name to the Family Planning Association, which gave its work a more positive slant. Trudie had always felt this was its goal: to help young men and women plan their families so there was not too much stress on the health of the mother or the family finances, thus giving the children a better start in life.

Trudie once told her niece that the role of the chairman was to 'get the views of the silent ones and to stop the others discussing items which are not on the agenda.' She needed all her skills in managing the meetings of the Birth Control Council, her chief difficulty being Dr Marie Stopes, whose dogmatic and emotional approach to any subject was diametrically opposed to Trudie's objective and practical viewpoint. While she did her best to accommodate Dr Stopes's attitudes and opinions, it was a relief when the good doctor resigned from the association in 1933.

Lady Denman was, of course, an extremely wealthy woman, but she only saw money as something that was useful because it allowed her to live comfortably and to financially support the causes she became involved in. She felt that riches carried with them the responsibility for their wise and careful use. She strongly disliked ostentation or extravagance. She saved – or rather, did not spend – much of her income in the 1920s and 1930s and so was able to meet the cost of running Balcombe House even after the Second World War, when income tax was 19s 6d in the pound. Her son became estranged from the family, but her daughter Judith married and had four children, who were a great delight to Trudie.

In 1936, she and Margaret Pyke were enjoying a golfing holiday in the south of France when she developed appendicitis. This then turned to peritonitis and was mismanaged by the French doctors who attended her. Against the odds, she survived the bungling of the doctors and the subsequent operation needed to put right their mistakes, commenting, 'What a good advertisement for smoking and drinking too much!'

She was pleased to have survived the ordeal because while she was convalescing, plans were sent through to her from the Land Settlement Association for cottages that were to be built with outside lavatories. She insisted on the lavatories being installed inside the houses because, as she pointed out, more people died of pneumonia in the country than in the slums, and having to visit outside lavatories might well be a contributing factor. She received so many letters from well wishers that Grace Hadow wrote to her, 'I can think of no-one outside royalty – and major royalty at that – about whom so many people would be so genuinely and warmly concerned.' From this point on her health was compromised, though she lived until 1954, when, after undergoing an operation to put right problems which had arisen from her first serious illness in 1935, she died of heart failure.

Everyone seems to agree that Lady Denman had a genius for organisation. She had a penetrating eye, and was intolerant of dishonesty, pomposity and pretension. Her occasional sharpness of tongue was offset by her kindness, and she had a rare sympathy with anyone lacking confidence. One VCO, a Mrs Freeman, recounts a story that shows Lady Denman's ability to recognise the worth of the quieter members of an organisation. Most VCOs were middle-class women, but one was appointed whose husband was a gardener – she was a working-class woman, lacking, as she herself saw it, the education to carry out her work or contribute to the general discussion at national level. When telling about her first encounter with Lady Denman, she says Lady Denman took her to task for looking so frightened. 'When we adjourned for lunch she asked me what was the matter. I said, "You are all educated people and I have no proper education or anything. I can't see what use I am going to be on this committee." She said, "You'll be as much use as any of us. Education doesn't mean a thing. It's experience that counts. We go down the village streets and see all the nice doorways but we don't know what goes on behind them. This is what we need to know: what sort of life the village people have got because we want to do as much as we can.'"

Trudie Denman was also deeply affectionate towards family, friends and colleagues. She was, by her own admission, rather reserved. 'I do not find it easy to express what I feel. I am thankful for the opportunity I have had of working with and for country women,' she said, when she retired from the chairmanship of the NFWI. On her death, people spoke of her formidable personality, offset by her quick sympathy and humour. Lady Brunner said, 'No-one could more clearly detect the danger and pitfalls in the path of a movement pledged to being non-party-political and non-sectarian, her kindness, her splendid honesty, her refusal to compromise and her pleasure in the young.'

4

A REALLY GOOD WOMAN:
GRACE HADOW

Another important person in the development of the WI was Grace Hadow, who became the vice-chairman to Lady Denman's chairman. They worked together for the good of the movement for twenty years, until Grace Hadow's untimely death in 1940.

Grace Eleanor Hadow was born to Revd William Hadow and his wife Mary, in South Cerney in Gloucestershire in December 1875, the youngest of six children. Her eldest brother, Harry, sixteen years her senior, was appointed her godfather. At that time the family were relatively poor, when compared to the likes of the Cowdreys, but, recalling those times, Mrs Hadow said, 'I used to put food and education first; other things like clothes matter only for the time being.' So Grace spent much of her childhood wearing cut-down versions of the mother's old clothes. Playing with her older brothers gave Grace a distaste for games considered right for little girls. She would rather help her brother Gerald with his collections of insects than sit at home sewing. She was educated at home until the age of thirteen, when she was sent to a boarding school near Stroud, where she stayed until she was fifteen. Her mother then removed her and she was sent to Truro High School, where her uncle, Archdeacon Cornish, lived, whose wife was a friend of the headmistress, Miss Arnold. Miss Arnold had been influenced by the teaching of Miss Beale (1831–1905), a keen suffragist and one of the founder members of the Kensington Society, which became the London Society for Women's Suffrage. Miss Beale was also principal of Cheltenham Ladies' College and founder of St Hilda's College, University of Oxford. There was a verse, well known to students, about Miss Beale and her friend and colleague Miss Buss, a pioneer of women's education, head of Camden High School for Girls, a suffragist and participant in the Kensington Society:

> Miss Buss and Miss Beale
> Cupid's darts do not feel.
> How different from us
> Miss Beale and Miss Buss.

Grace was very influenced by Miss Arnold and became very fond of her. Miss Arnold took the long view. 'The importance of education consists in its effect on character,' said Miss Arnold. 'To train in unselfishness, in devotion to truth, in self-control, is more difficult than to train the reason and memory; it is also more important; it is not for success in the next examination that we are teaching, it is not even in success in their future career that we train these children; ... we are looking to eternity for the judgement on our work.'

Grace left Truro in 1894 but maintained contact with her mother's family. She became an ardent sailor, taught by her brother-in-law John Cornish. She then took up a post at Cheltenham Ladies'

College, Miss Beale's sphere of influence, on the understanding that she had some time to prepare for the entrance exam for Oxford University, the 'Women's First'. The exam for women differed from that for the men in that the languages they were examined in were French and German rather than Latin and Greek. Women had been allowed to attend lectures at the Oxford colleges and even take exams but couldn't be awarded a degree because they had not been allowed to matriculate, i.e. become full members of the university. This right was granted in 1920 and Grace Hadow graduated in 1922. The hour allotted to her for private study at Cheltenham started at 6.30 a.m., which was not the most helpful of arrangements, and she was probably relieved to go up to Somerville College in 1900 to read English Language and Literature.

Her brother and godfather W. E. Hadow, or Harry, was long established in the city, having been a student, lecturer and appointed Dean of Worcester College in 1889. Grace found a ready-made social life among Harry's circle. The women studying in Oxford at that time, too, formed such a small group with such similar interests that it must have been easy to feel at home there.

Among the friends she made and the people she met were people who were not only clever and articulate, but also liberal in outlook. Some of them were passionate about women's education, others were passionate about women's rights and concerned with tackling the social evils that beset the country. One of her fellow students at Somerville, Helen Darbishire, who eventually became principal of Somerville, was a literary scholar specialising in Wordsworth and Milton. She was from a Manchester family who were at the centre of the Liberal and Unitarian Society there.

Grace showed an early interest in amateur dramatics when she and some of her friends appeared in an amateur production of *Everyman*, with Grace as Everyman, Helen Darbishire as Good Deeds and Eleanor Lodge as Kindred. A late medieval morality play, to modern eyes it looks terribly worthy and rather static, but it is still performed today, so there must be some merit in it and the photograph of the performance shows the young women with their hair loose, which was probably rather daring. The play shows Everyman in conversation with Death and only able to be accompanied in the Afterlife by Good Deeds. The performance shows that Grace Hadow was interested in drama, an interest she would support and foster among WI branches rather later in her life.

Eleanor Rathbone, campaigner for women's rights, who later became an MP and argued for a family allowance to be paid to the mother of a household, was also at Oxford at this time, as was Margery Fry, who following the 1914–18 war became involved in penal reform, became a Justice of the Peace, education adviser to Holloway Prison and later principal of Somerville. These friends and acquaintances – clever, well-educated people with a social conscience, who were very aware of the shortcomings of their society – had a driving ambition to improve life for their less-fortunate fellow citizens, and inspired Grace Hadow to want to serve the society she lived in.

Of course Grace was not only influenced by her friends and acquaintances, she in turn influenced others, and one family she affected to a great degree was the Deneke family. The Deneke sisters, Helena and Margaret, were the daughters of a German banker and his wife, Clara. Much to Helena's father's bemusement – he is reputed to have asked, 'Why do you want to go and live among a lot of clever women?' – Helena decided to study English at St Hugh's College. This was in 1900, and as both she and Grace were studying the same subject, though Grace was at Somerville, they became firm friends. Following her time as a student at St Hugh's, Helena became a tutor in English there and later taught German, as well as being a librarian. When Helena moved to Lady Margaret Hall, Mr Deneke bought a house, Gunfield, right next door to the college.

The Denekes made Gunfield into a cultural centre, receiving such honoured guests as Albert Schweitzer and Albert Einstein to their evening parties, and having musical soirees at which Margaret, a well-known pianist, performed. When Grace Hadow started working in Oxford in the 1920s she lived with the Denekes, and became very fond of the whole family. The name of Helena, or Lena, as she was known to her friends, keeps cropping up in the story of the WI, not directly, because no-one ever thought to write her biography, but incidentally, in snippets of information in the WI magazine *Home and Country*, in the minute books of Elsfield WI and among the letters sent to the Oxfordshire Federation in 1940. I think she was the sort of stalwart, unassuming woman, not given to self-advertisement, that was typical of many of the women in the WI.

Following her time at Somerville as a student, Grace spent another brief time in America, but she returned to Oxford in 1903 to take up a temporary post at Somerville. She then transferred to a more permanent position at Lady Margaret Hall (LMH), where she became its first resident English tutor. Lady Margaret Hall was High Church, and at that time was under the principalship of Elizabeth Wordsworth, no friend of women's suffrage. Though a great scholar, Miss Wordsworth thought the main role of a woman, however intelligent and educated she was, should be as wife and mother, though she, of course, was neither. Eleanor Lodge was also a tutor at Lady Margaret Hall, and she and Grace undertook cycling tours together.

Grace inadvertently raised the standard of accommodation for tutors because she needed two rooms – a bedroom and a sitting room – since etiquette forbad her to receive a man in her room, even if he were her brother! She trained the LMH choir and established herself as a scholar of English, publishing a book entitled *The Oxford Treasury of Verse* with her brother. She played tennis with Eleanor Lodge and gave luncheon parties once a week at Worcester College with her brother. She was living life to the full.

Then in 1909 her mother fell ill, and Grace was faced with the kind of dilemma that confronts many women today – whether to assume her family responsibilities or continue with her career. She managed a sort of compromise. She initially gave up residence at LMH, though she continued as a tutor there for a while. Two years later she resigned the tutorship and became a visiting lecturer, spending two days a week at LMH. This must have inevitably affected her academic career, but as we shall see, her talents were later put to very good use in other ways. She lived in Cirencester for most of the week, caring for her mother, who had moved there following the death of her husband. Mrs Hadow was a Conservative. Opposed to women's suffrage, she called Gladstone, the Liberal Prime Minister, 'England's scourge' and a radical government, according to Helena Deneke, she deemed nothing short of 'wicked'. She was against giving women the vote, as was Grace's brother Harry. Though aware of the price she paid by taking on the responsibility of her mother, Grace would say, 'There is always someone else who can do other things equally well, but no-one else can do this particular thing.'

She must have been lonely in Cirencester, though Eleanor Lodge did cycle over from time to time to see her. There were few people interested in the things that interested her, few people interested in women's suffrage. She nevertheless joined and became secretary of the local branch of the National Union of Women's Suffrage Societies (NUWSS), though this did nothing to add to her popularity in the neighbourhood. In 1917 when women's suffrage was looking likely, she wrote,

> It feels quite odd to think that possibly – even probably – before long people will neither shout with laughter nor throw things at one if one mentions women voting. I am glad to belong to a generation which has been stoned – not because I like being stoned. It is tiresome, and often messy, but since some women had to go through that to win the thing, it is a bit of luck not to have been out of it entirely ... In years to come it may interest people to realise that before the War numbers of law-abiding and peaceful women like myself, quite inconspicuous members of a political party, got to take being mobbed and insulted as part of the ordinary day's work.

She was, however, against militant suffragettes, who she thought provoked the trouble. She sent her congratulations to Mrs Fawcett, President of the NUWSS, when the Women's Suffrage Clause passed the House of Lords in the Franchise Bill of 1918 with a majority of sixty-nine, and Mrs Fawcett's reply was one of the few letters she kept. She stayed clear of party politics, however, and called herself an 'individualist anarchist'.

While in Cirencester she started a girls' club which put on plays. She also arranged concerts through her Oxford contacts and even preached in a Nonconformist chapel. Her skills as a speaker and her organisational skills began to be appreciated. A local tradesmen's meeting on some public matter elected her to take the chair, which would be unusual even today. She kept up with her academic work to some extent, translating Berthold Litzman's *Life of Clara Schumann*, and she wrote on *Chaucer and his Times* for the Home University series of publications.

When war broke out she became involved in work with Belgian refugees and in supporting British troops by sending food parcels to prisoners of war in Germany, writing to them. She offered to teach soldiers elementary French before they embarked for the war, and also organised the knitting of blankets for POWs. She put an appeal for odds and ends of knitting wool in the *Daily Graphic* and was astonished at the quantity she received – nineteen to twenty parcels a time. 'Wool from every part of the United Kingdom. I distribute sacksful of it and still it overflows a large clothes basket: all this in odd half balls and scraps left over from knitting,' she wrote. 'I have already sent off fourteen "blankets" and the lightest weighs over two lbs.'

She tracked the change in women's position in society with great interest. She rejoiced in Dr Rosalie Jobson's report about how she and her associates, the seven members of the Women's Hospital Corps, though rejected by the English War Office, had been funded by the NUWSS and accepted in France and the Balkans, where their surgery met a great need. She heard at first hand how Dr Alice Hutchinson had smuggled the Union Jack under her blouse in the retreat from Serbia. She was also interested to see how women were working as ticket collectors and clerks on the Great Western Railway. She received news of her friend Helena Deneke, who had taken time off from her job as bursar at LMH, for which she had no qualifications and little aptitude, to work with suffrage relief projects in France.

Grace herself must have longed for the opportunity to become more involved with the splendid work the suffrage societies were doing on the Continent, but she had to content herself with working for the War Agricultural Committee, who were asking for volunteers to work on the land. Soon Grace was speaking at agricultural meetings in different parts of the country and found that in many instances women were already banding together to work on the allotments abandoned by their husbands, or forming collective poultry farms. In February 1916 she wrote, 'I've just been elected a member of the Gloucestershire Chamber of Agriculture. A very odd effect of the war on an Oxford teacher.'

Grace saw the effects of women doing farm work and was full of admiration and respect for both individuals and the work they achieved. She wrote about 'women of all sorts and kinds brought together by their own desire to work for their country where work is needed', an impulse from which the Women's Institute grew.

Grace founded one of the earliest branches in the country when she started the Cirencester WI. Her mother's journal records, 'July 10, 1916. The Women's Institute established. Grace President and chief speaker.' She notes in her own diary in February 1917 that 'Sapperton has formed its own branch. A campaign is being held to form Women's Institutes throughout the country and I went to start one there. We had an exhibition of war-food – really delicious barley bread and oat cake and parkin, an excellent address on rations from the sister of a neighbouring vicar.'

By April of that year as a response to food shortages she helped to found the Cirencester and District Food Production Committee, with a view to organising increased production of vegetables and fruit and the co-operative marketing of these valuable foodstuffs. 'We have founded seventeen Women's Institutes in surrounding villages and the women are really eager to try new methods and to experiment with war breads etc. The movement ought to do a great deal not only to promote thrift but to educate country women and to improve conditions of village life.'

About the time she was writing this, her mother died. After that event she saw no reason to stay in Cirencester. She resigned her post at LMH and decided to look for full-time war work. Rather surprisingly, given that she was an academic who specialised in English poetry, she was offered the directorship of a subsection of the Ministry of Munitions, a section of the Welfare Department. It was concerned with the health and welfare of women munitions workers employed in both national and private munitions factories, nationwide. There was no national welfare service, so this was something of an experiment.

Research in 1915 had established that overwork and poor working conditions had contributed, unsurprisingly, to the poor health of the workers. As a result of this realisation, Seebohm Rowntree was invited to head the Welfare Department. Seebohm Rowntree had conducted what amounted to the first sociological survey in Britain. He had made society aware that poverty existed throughout the country, that it was caused by a lack of income often due to the wage earner being paid a pittance, ideas which now seem so commonplace as hardly to need stating, but which were new at the time. He also established the idea of a poverty line, which marked the difference between being able to live reasonably and having to do without the necessities of life. The department he headed and where Grace Hadow worked concerned itself with almost anything which affected the welfare of the workers: lodgings, housing conditions, crèches, clubs, travel to work and maternity homes.

In the course of her work Grace visited factories, addressed munitions workers and took part in educational activities for workers. She mentions in one of her letters that she gave a lecture on nature poetry – with no lantern slides, nothing to help it down – and attracted an audience of 500 men and women. Grace was astonished. She had never talked to a more responsive audience. 'They were quite a rough type,' she writes, 'and my heart was in my boots when I began, especially as I had been told the employer's point of view was that no sane person could expect factory hands to listen to stuff like that. And they came to such an extent that there was no standing room. How's that for the working man and woman after a hard day's work!' She was, it has to be said, a charismatic and very entertaining speaker.

On 13 July 1918 she attended a service at St Paul's, attended by the king and queen, for munitions workers, 134 of whom had been killed and 250 injured the previous week in an explosion at National Filling Station number six at Chilwell in Nottinghamshire. (The 'filling' bit meant filling bombs with explosive.) The blast was heard twenty miles away. The chemicals used by the women working at the factory caused their skin to turn yellow, so they were known locally as the Chilwell Canaries. In its working life from 1916 to 1918 the factory produced some 19 million shells, 50 per cent of all the shells fired during the war. Of the service at St Paul's, Grace writes,

Looking from the choir on that great mass of men was curiously moving and the Last Post made me think of the 200 killed and wounded and their comrades who were back at work the next day. The Lord Mayor attended in state and the Bishop covered with orders and medals and somewhere, I suppose, the King and Queen. But it was the congregation that counted.

In October of the same year she was 'lent' to the USA to exchange ideas about the work and role of the YWCA. News of the armistice reached her in Oklahoma City, where she was woken in the middle of the night by a cacophony of sounds generated by enthusiastic revellers, banging tin lids and shovels, hooting motors, blowing whistles, and one 'staid elderly woman walking round the hotel ringing a dinner bell'. She spoke to every and any group who wanted to listen, and they were keen to hear her war stories and descriptions of air raids. She asked to attend a black church, where she found a warm welcome and very much appreciated the quality of the singing. She came home in December to the imminent disbandment of the Department of Munitions – she would soon be out of a job.

The war had brought a great many changes, not least the movement of women out of the home and into the workplace. Some of them had aspirations they would follow now the war was over. Grace Hadow had great expectations of the change. As one girl who had been a servant before the war expressed it, 'Four of us were the only girls allowed to set up our own tools in the shop. We used to swank a bit. I don't mind cooking, but if I cook I want to train and be a first-rate one, not just an ordinary general.' Grace thought this attitude could be fostered, to the benefit of women and the society they lived and worked in.

Grace may not have been able to dash out to France to help the women doctors there, but her experiences during the war years had given her knowledge of a wider world than academia and the country life of Cirencester. Because of her contacts with factory workers, refugees and POWs she had gained not only new insights into human behaviour, but respect for working men and women whose lives were far from easy. She had also learnt how to be a good administrator and had honed her skills as a speaker. She was convinced that people had a thirst for knowledge and for culture that their lives, as then lived, did not fulfil.

On 3 October 1916 the Women's Institute subcommittee of the Agricultural Organisation Society had decided to ask Lady Denman to become chairman, and, if she consented, to ask the Board of Agriculture to appoint her as one of the governors of the AOS. Under the leadership of Lady Denman, the Women's Institute subcommittee of the AOS proposed the setting up of the central committee of management of Women's Institutes, which would consist of some officially appointed members but a majority of representatives of the institutes. Lady Denman was of course the chairman of this organisation, and in 1918 Grace Hadow was elected vice-chairman. It was Grace herself who moved the resolution by which the central committee of the Women's Institutes gained its independence from the AOS. It was she who devised the constitution of the WI, laying down the structure we know today. She had several models she could have followed. She had experience of the Church, since her father was a vicar, and of government bureaucracy, as she had worked for the Ministry of War. She had chaired meetings of local businessmen in Cirencester and had experience of the university college system. She also had experience of the chaotic world of the suffrage movement, where groups formed, splintered, and re-formed, energy that could more usefully have been put towards furthering the cause.

She must have been keen to avoid this sort of situation, having seen how unproductive it could be. She wanted to educate the membership not just in the skills they needed in their work, but in how to become part of the democratic process. To do this, people had to be able to practise making decisions, which meant voting at branch level on how the branch should be run, and discussing how they wanted to 'build a better Britain'. These decisions needed to be passed up the organisation to the people at the top, who would lobby government ministers on behalf of the members. Branches and county federations were already up and running, with the pattern at branch level already set by Madge Watt. The structure of the WI as set up by Grace Hadow has a great deal in common with another body set up at the time – the Trades Union Congress. They were confronted with a similar situation: how to channel the opinions of a large number of members at grass-roots level into a coherent policy for the organisation as a whole.

Though there have been modifications over the years, the general structure of the WI is largely still as Grace Hadow set it up. Each institute is self-governing and elects its own committee by secret ballot. The branch meets at least once a month and institutes are grouped into county federations, which have an executive committee elected for no more than two years. The county federation's job is to co-ordinate the work of institutes in their area and to act as a channel of communication with the executive committee of the National Federation of Women's Institutes. They must also seek to provide instruction, training and other facilities for members. At least once a year there has to be a county council meeting of delegates elected by the institutes. The aim of the national executive is to foster unity of purpose among member institutes and county federations and to communicate with government and other authorities on the institutes' behalf. On the national executive committee are seventeen elected WI members, four co-opted WI members, including one Welsh speaker, as well as representatives of the Ministry of Agriculture, the DHSS, and the Department of Education. Twice a year there is a national council meeting where the chairmen and treasurers of the county federations meet with the national executive to discuss policy. At one of these, the resolutions submitted by institutes or federations are considered for acceptance on the agenda of the AGM. Resolutions are the means by which national policy is formed. They are the political and social issues which may be acted on at local, federation or national level.

This constitution resulted in an organisation which allows a great deal of freedom to individual branches – they can talk about what they like, providing it is not party political, they can arrange what they want to do, they can join in county organised events or not, they can spend the whole time having tea parties if they so wish. But a very tight control is kept on the political direction the organisation takes, because the policy is set by resolutions which admittedly come from the branches, but which are then selected by the national executive. This means that any resolutions that may be politically sensitive can be weeded out. Because of the people who were originally appointed to, or invited to join, the NFWI, and subsequently the people who worked their way up the organisation, there was an inbuilt tendency to conservatism. It was generally suffragists who found their way to the WI, not the suffragettes, and Grace Hadow and people like her wanted to work co-operatively, not confrontationally. In addition, the way people such as Phyllis Wickham were recruited meant that new recruits were moulded to the organisation by older members, perhaps before they had the experience to be innovative. Grace Hadow, however, could not be expected to see fifty years into the future. She dealt with the problems of organising a nationwide federation very successfully for the time.

She returned to Oxford in 1920 wanting to do some kind of

social work. As Helena Deneke puts it, 'She had the building of a better England very much at heart.' She was convinced of the need for the development of responsible citizenship, which she saw as something linked to the recently gained women's suffrage. The Representation of the People Act of 1918 had given the vote to women over thirty with minimum property qualifications, though it was a further ten years before the age was lowered to twenty-one.

On her return to civilian life, Grace was offered and accepted the secretaryship of Barnett House, in Oxford, which had been founded in 1914. Understandably, given people's preoccupation with the war effort, the project had achieved very little. It had been conceived as a centre of information on social and economic issues, and its functions were to collect a library for this purpose, to provide lectures on particular aspects of these issues, and to provide training courses for social service, there being no such department in the university. Grace was attracted to the post because she would be given a free hand to develop the service as she saw fit, and she could use the experience she had gained in her other work to make Barnett House a success. She saw immediately that she could use this post to increase the resources available to the rural economy, thus benefitting local branches of the WI. Barnett House was intended to be a centre for social and economic studies and social-work training. It was not her aim, she said, to take folk dancing and travelling cinemas to outlying villages, but 'to get people to formulate their own demands and tackle problems.'

One of the prime movers in the scheme was Professor W. G. S. Adams, who was keen to see improvements in farming and food production. Grace was appointed to the secretaryship in 1920, and the organising council accepted Professor Adams' scheme to place the facilities of Barnett House at the disposal of villages within thirty miles of Oxford. They also agreed that there should be close co-operation with certain voluntary organisations, the Workers' Educational Association (WEA), the Young Men's Christian Association (YMCA) and the Women's Institutes. To prevent duplication of effort Grace drew together representatives of these rural organisations along with the Village Clubs Association (VCA), which had been started at the end of the war to help people settle back into rural life by providing more lively village events. Grace became an early member of the executive committee of the National Council of Social Services, founded in 1919. It is now known as the National Council for Voluntary Organisations, and is an umbrella body for voluntary organisations. In 1919 it was concerned to promote co-operation rather than competition as a way forward. Grace was one of the first to see how this principle might be applied to the countryside. She dealt with rural policy, and from the group of voluntary bodies with which she was involved – the WEA, the WI, the Village Clubs and the YMCA – the Oxfordshire Rural Community Council was formed. She wrote, 'We are trying to build up a finer and better England and to do so on a sure foundation of mutual helpfulness, self-respect and extension of knowledge. Isn't that worth working for?'

This emphasis on co-operation between groups meant that one group of volunteers might well be able to provide expertise for another group. Commander Kettlewell, for instance, a leader in the Village Clubs movement, was also a supporter of the WI, his wife being President of Burford WI, and he gave lectures at the V&A on the principals of banner design, himself designing the banners of Carterton and Clanfield WIs.

At this time Oxfordshire County Council had turned down the offer of a Carnegie grant to start a county library that would ultimately be paid for from the rates, in the belief that 'Oxfordshire people don't want to read'! Grace Hadow's response was, 'We must prove that Oxfordshire people do want to read.' The YMCA made their collection of books available, about a hundred books housed in a dozen boxes, and other books were either bought or given, and were kept in Grace Hadow's office at Barnett House because there was nowhere else to put them. A dilapidated black Ford van was eventually acquired and driven by Mr A. G. H. Griffiths, who took books and lecturers out to the villages. A pioneer wireless set would travel round on the roof of the van and Mr Griffiths would demonstrate this wonder of modern technology to awestruck villagers. The van was eventually replaced with a snub-nosed Morris called Andrew (after Andrew Carnegie), which was often driven by Grace herself. In 1923, after much campaigning, the WI helped persuade Oxfordshire County Council to support libraries. The village library collected at Barnett House was taken over by the county council, the librarian, Miss Mackintosh, becoming the first county librarian. Barnett House was also involved with music and drama, providing good plays for amateurs to perform, and channelling Carnegie grants to the appropriate recipients.

Grace Hadow remained secretary of Barnett House until 1929, when she was asked to become principal of the Society for Home Students. There were four women's colleges already established in Oxford: Lady Margaret Hall, established in 1878, Somerville in 1879, St Hugh's in 1886 and St Hilda's in 1893. There were also a considerable number of students who lived in private lodgings, and it was to look after the interests of these students that the Society of Home Students had been established. The post of principal was not an easy one, because not only had she to get to know and be responsive to the needs of the home students, she also had to contact and keep an eye on their hostesses, to ensure standards were maintained. Grace Hadow was a great principal, according to her biographer, Helena Deneke. 'She accepted and revered the living part of the traditions she inherited, yet she interpreted them within the light of present circumstances, and laid a foundation for development on firm, clear lines,' says Miss Deneke. Money for the organisation was always in short supply, and it was to help provide funds for the establishment of St Anne's College, which grew out of the Society for Home Students, that she undertook her last lecture tour to America.

In her leisure time Grace played as hard as she worked. In the summer she went climbing in the Alps, conquering several of the Alpine peaks, including the Matterhorn, sleeping in mountain huts, camping out, climbing, and cutting steps in the glacier ice by the light of a lantern. She also had hair-raising holidays in the Balkans, making her way down the Adriatic as far as Albania. Wherever she went she collected postcards and took photographs to use in her talks when she came back to England.

The last years of the 1930s saw a series of setbacks for Grace. In 1937 her brother Harry died, with Grace at his side, and in 1938 she embarked on a long and extremely tiring lecture tour in the USA to raise funds for the Society of Home Students back in Oxford. 'I'm leading an odd life,' she wrote,

I spend anything from eight to fourteen hours in the stuffiest of trains and arrive either early in the morning or in the late afternoon at some unknown place. Usually someone meets me and takes me to the Hotel or private house where I am to stay. I am supposed to give one lecture of about an hour, but frequently as I go round the college I'm asked if I'd mind addressing a group of students then and there, or saying a few words to a class. Then they mention casually that there is a luncheon party at which it is hoped I will speak and after lunch a special meeting has been called of the local branch of the Institute of International Affairs: will I talk to it about Czechoslovakia? So I've a busy day!

At the end of her tour she made her way to Toronto to meet up with Helena Deneke. She had been asked to speak to the University Women's Club and found herself confronted with an audience of 2,000. From there she went to Ottawa to stay with the Governor-General of Canada and his wife. They were the novelist and politician John Buchan, recently ennobled so he could take up the prestigious job of governor, and his wife Susie, erstwhile President of Elsfield WI. Everyone at Government House was shocked to see how tired she looked. She left Ottawa on the *Duchess of Richmond*, the last boat to sail down the St Lawrence that year. Helena Deneke writes that she never really recovered from that lecture tour.

The following year she intended to have a relaxing holiday in Poland, but the political situation was such that that was impossible, so she settled for a trip to Norway with Miss Deneke in the hopes of some mountain walking. While there they met an Englishman who invited them to listen to the wireless he had chartered for the evening. They heard Lord Halifax's speech on the eve of war and decided to hurry home, catching the last boat before war was declared. Grace was very much involved with the evacuation of London schools to Oxfordshire, and for Christmas

1939 she travelled to Carlisle in great discomfort, having to stand the whole way. From there she travelled to London in the New Year, where she intended to do some work but also have a little leisure time with Helena Deneke. When Miss Deneke arrived she found her friend in bed with a sore throat, which quickly turned to pneumonia. The new M and B tablets helped a little, but she could not fight off the infection, and died two weeks later on 19 January 1940. She must have died a very disappointed woman. She must have thought all she had worked so hard for in the previous twenty years could well be destroyed. All her beliefs in working co-operatively, not confrontationally, her vision for a happier, fairer world, all had come to nothing.

When she died Lady Denman said, 'How shall we manage without her?' She gave a moving testimony to Grace Hadow's many qualities.

> I remember how her quickness in seeing the essential point of whatever was being discussed and her most entertaining comments made these early committee meetings stimulating and interesting. I was startled when I discovered her academic record. I could not believe that anyone of Miss Hadow's knowledge could give serious consideration to the views of anyone as ignorant as myself. I never really got used to Miss Hadow's humility of mind and during the long years of our association I was impressed by the way in which she received suggestions from us all. ... I do not think that she herself ever realised or appreciated that she had unique gifts both as a speaker and a writer.

Her funeral was at the university church of St Mary the Virgin in the High Street in Oxford, where the congregation sang 'Jerusalem', and there is a plaque there to remember her by.

5

BUILDING A BETTER BRITAIN:
THE INTER-WAR YEARS

Grace Hadow said WI members must 'learn to realise their responsibility towards the community in which they live, and from an interest in their own village and their own county, come to see the connection between their affairs and those of the nation at large'. This chapter tells the story of how in the inter-war years one village, Elsfield, did just that.

The village of Elsfield is at the top of a hill three miles from the centre of Oxford, and has been there since Saxon times. In the 1920s and 1930s there was a small collection of about forty cottages, four farms, a manor house, a vicarage, a school and a church. The parish was bought in 1919 by the Oxford University college of Christ Church, who immediately sold the manor, its accompanying cottages and several acres of land to John Buchan, who with his wife and four children moved in almost immediately. The following year Susan Buchan organised her first Women's Institute meeting.

One of the reasons for the success of the branch, I think, was its proximity to Oxford, where there were so many resources available:

Barnett House with its library, not only of books, but also of plays that could be borrowed, New College, which provided an easily accessible venue for yearly events, and above all, the people. Susan Buchan, of course, and her husband, but also the Deneke sisters, Helena, who joined Elsfield WI in 1927, and Margaret, who was a well-known pianist. After the founding of Denman College, Margaret played the piano regularly in the evening to entertain students there. Helena took an active part in running the branch, driving up to Elsfield from her home in North Oxford, and was a founder member of the Oxfordshire Federation. Grace Hadow came to talk on her travels in Europe, and John Buchan, one of the first WI husbands to be drawn in to the federation's activities, was often co-opted to take part in pageants or act as a teller when there was an election.

Susan Buchan had arrived in Elsfield with little experience of life in the country beyond what she had gleaned from Mary Webb's *Gone to Earth*. Mary Webb wrote fiction, and Mrs Buchan soon realised that life as she had envisaged it in the country was far removed from reality.

> Like many town-dwellers of that day, I thought of life in the country as picturesque, stark and extremely romantic. I soon discovered I must spin the romance for myself as the village dwellers saw none in their lives or surroundings and that they regarded moonlight, sunsets, the hush of a December evening and the splendour of a lilac-scented May morning with equal indifference.

I think she misread the villagers' reluctance to talk about such things as a lack of appreciation of the beauty around them. But be that as it may, she found the villagers completely turned in on themselves. The gossip and intrigues were difficult to come to terms with and she decided that life in a village was rather like life on board ship, by which I think she must have meant those interminable journeys to and from India, where nothing much happened. 'You are all in it together,' she wrote, 'and human beings in a situation such as this watch each other closely, pounce on their neighbours' defects and are always sceptical about any sign of improvement.' Locked in together with no escape!

As a newcomer and a Londoner at that, Mrs Buchan's attempts to improve village life were met with suspicion at first. Miss Parsons, who had been born and had lived at the manor all her life until her brother sold the estate to Christ Church, was understandably wary. Mrs Buchan records that Miss Parsons would have done anything for the people of Elsfield. She had, after all, supervised the girls' needlework and provided material for pinafores in the little village school, she had watched and photographed the men at work in her father's fields. She knew everyone, their strengths and weaknesses, and their family history. To be asked to be part of an organisation that had democracy at its very core, with everyone expected to contribute in equal measure, was not easy, and Susan Buchan pays tribute to that. She writes,

It is greatly to Miss Parsons' credit that she became such an admirable Institute member. The idea ran completely counter to all her prejudices and established principles ... The Women's Institute, with its democratic set-up, and its accent on the members expressing their opinions freely, and running everything themselves, was a strange new portent to her.

In her book *The Acceptable Face of Feminism*, Maggie Andrews asserts that the WI saw itself as the epitome of Englishness. Village life should be a model of co-operative working, service to others and class conciliation, rather than confrontation and exploitation, and Mrs Buchan's comments bear this out. Susan Buchan's heart must have been in her mouth as she waited to see if anyone would turn up to that first meeting. She could expect that Miss Parsons, suspicious as she was of such new-fangled notions, would come out of a sense of class solidarity, and similarly Mrs Elkington, the vicar's wife. Miss Hopcraft, the teacher, could be expected to come along from her tiny thatched cottage standing alongside the school. She no doubt expected that Mrs Gentelia Webb, wife of their chauffeur Amos, who lived in one of their cottages, would come – she would hardly dare to stay away. But what about Mrs Hambidge, who kept the village shop and whose eight children took up a great deal of her time, what about Mrs Bedding, who had lost her son when his ship had been torpedoed in 1915? What of Mrs Paintin, whose husband was a labourer who earned extra money as a knacker?

She need not have worried. At the very first meeting of the branch, held at the manor at 3 p.m. on 4 May 1920, thirty-three people attended. She had thought about a talk on beekeeping as something suitably rustic. Bees seemed to feature rather a lot in Mary Webb's books. When she had suggested this to various people in the village there had been no opposition. It was only via Mrs Elkington that the news filtered through to her that people were not interested in bees. There were two beekeepers in the village already; the people who didn't keep bees didn't want to know about them and if they did they would ask the people who already kept them. The logic was impeccable, but why hadn't they said so? It was the beginning of a journey for both Mrs Buchan and the women of the village. She began to understand why they were passive and uncommunicative, and they learnt to express their views without rancour and realised that their opinions would be valued and acted upon.

There was no doubting who would be elected president. Until she had to leave Elsfield in 1935 to go to Canada with her husband, who had been made Governor-General, Susan Buchan was chosen every year. She did, however, earn the confidence that the branch placed in her. It was her idea, so she had a personal stake in its success, and for the first three years she delivered notices to the members herself. In 1924 this had become rather too much and the treasurer, Mrs Clinkard, wife of one of the farm managers, sold twopenny notebooks so members could write down information about future meetings. Mrs Buchan, along with Miss Parsons, was also generous with financial support, providing prizes for competitions, tickets for events such as a trip to London Zoo, and American cloth for the table. And even if lifts in her car could be something of an ordeal, given the strong smell of petrol from the cans carried in the boot, since petrol stations were few and far between, and even if the smell of John Buchan's Turkish cigarettes was rather more than you could stomach, it was still easier for many women than plodding up or down the hill to Oxford, three miles away. The competition prizes on offer were useful and were appreciated by participants: Brasso, tea, soap, tinned fish. Prizes in the Christmas draw in 1930 were similarly practical and generous: a boy's woollen suit, half a ton of coal, a Christmas cake, a turkey, a cockerel, plum pudding, bottle of wine and the ubiquitous cigarettes. Prizes worth winning!

The idea of voting for something in a secret ballot must have seemed a novel and exciting idea. No more lobbying, or having your ideas dismissed as irrelevant or stupid. You were entitled to think and vote according to your own opinions, even if that vote was only cast to determine who should be treasurer or president of the branch. It also encouraged people to think about matters and to make their own judgements and decisions, all of which would be useful when it came to voting in government elections. And perhaps most importantly of all, their opinions counted and were acted on. They were no longer merely passive observers of events; they could affect what would happen.

Other members of that first committee were the vicar's wife, Mrs Elkington, who became joint vice-president along with Miss Parsons. Alongside these middle- and even upper-class people were the chauffeur's wife Mrs Webb, and Mrs Allam, whose brother-in-law was the Buchans' gamekeeper. Mrs Charlett, the Buchans' cook, also soon joined the ranks of the WI.

Mrs Elkington provided the branch with cups and saucers until March 1921, when they decided to buy their own. They postponed their purchase of crockery until June of that year to see if prices came down, by which time they had £6 10s 11d in hand. They then bought three dozen cups and saucers (white), three dozen plates, four jugs for milk, six bread-and-butter plates and a dozen teaspoons. Miss Parsons offered to enamel everything with the WI logo, which would save a lot of money, and at this point Mrs Buchan gave the American cloth to cover the table. I find Susan Buchan and Miss Parsons' acceptance of the need to economise quite touching – they were women who were used to the best. Such sensitivity on their part must have been one of the factors in making the branch such a welcoming and lively place.

Food production had been one of the main reasons for the original foundation of the WI, so it might have been expected that there would have been more emphasis on food production at their monthly meetings. The emphasis seems, however, to have been on dressmaking and making things rather than food, though some of the speakers and competitions were based on food – growing it, keeping it and preparing it hygienically (no small problem in cottages where there was no running water). There were competitions for making rock cakes, cake baking, and how many potatoes they could grow from a single potato (donated by Mrs Buchan), which was won by Mrs Watts with eleven pounds eight ounces' worth of potatoes. Mrs Hambidge only managed to grow one pound, but Mrs Watts was a farmer's wife and had access to unlimited supplies of horse manure, which no doubt improved her chances. There was also a demonstration on trussing a chicken, which was poorly attended because it was raining cats and dogs. There was a blackberrying picnic and a demonstration of practical gardening. Mrs Allam always exhibited at the county federation shows and won certificates, not just for her vegetables, but for her wines. It may be that the women of Elsfield felt they had little to learn about growing vegetables, since their household budgets and family welfare depended on how much they and their husbands could grow. Even the smallest cottage had a huge garden with room to keep a pig and a few chickens, and a vegetable plot.

At the very first meeting of the WI in May 1919, Miss Parsons handed out small pieces of material to be made by the members into something useful for the July bazaar. Of course, Miss Parsons had supervised the girls' needlework at the school for many years and knew exactly who was capable of what. Susan Buchan attributes the branch's success in competitions and exhibitions almost entirely to Miss Parsons. She would look over her steel-rimmed spectacles and say, 'I have put you down for this for the

County Exhibition in two months' time.' As she went around the village from house to house collecting a household's contribution to the coal and clothing club, or the Radcliffe Infirmary, she would remind people of the contribution they had promised to the Elsfield WI entry to the exhibition. There was no escape. She herself did beautiful cross stitch and once won the Women's Institute award, the 'Gold Star', for a piece of cross stitch. In their very first year Elsfield entered items they had made in the Oxford Handicrafts Exhibition, winning four prizes, and in subsequent years they won the coveted shield for small institutes several times.

The emphasis the WI placed on competition may seem slightly odd to us today, but it served a very useful purpose. It provided a way of celebrating what women had achieved and was a permanent record of a woman's achievement, when so much of women's work at that time was repetitive and ephemeral. The bread was eaten as soon as it was made, the rice pudding gobbled up by hungry farm workers, the washing soaked, scrubbed, mangled, dried, ironed and put away, only to be succeeded by another lot of dirty clothes. Nothing stayed done. Making a rag rug, re-caning a chair or knitting a jumper was a permanent marker of women's work in the home. Mrs Webb gained national recognition for her cuddly hen, which sadly is not described, and which was admired by no less a person than the queen herself at an exhibition at Wembley.

The WI also used what were seen as traditional women's skills to demonstrate to the men how skilled they really were. At the Christmas socials, competitions were organised for the men in which they were expected to undertake tasks they were unfamiliar with. Hat trimming was one such task, as was darning stockings – Miss Hatt at Church Farm promised to provide the stockings.

One of the ways of making their presence felt was by making a banner expressing their collective sense of identity. In 1921 Mrs Buchan offered to make one and May Allam, who lived across from the manor, said she would like to help. May Allam's family was long-established in the village. Her father had been a groom for Miss Parsons' father before moving into the family business working as a carpenter and wheelwright, and her mother had been a dressmaker who had made up clothes for the village children from the material given them by Miss Parsons' mother.

The main piece of material in the banner, which looks suspiciously like the curtain material that might have adorned the sitting-room windows at the manor, is pale blue brocade with the pattern running sideways rather than vertically. On this is embroidered a black bird, a jackdaw, rather well embroidered, though the tree it is nesting in is less well represented and the coat of arms of Christ Church almost obliterates the tree trunk. The design is unimpressive, but it was at least Elsfield's own. Jackdaws were a ubiquitous presence in the woods near the manor. One had been known to steal parts of the manuscript of one of Buchan's books to line its nest. And there was at that time a very impressive double row of elm trees lining both sides of a large portion of the village street. People took a great deal of care to select images that would represent their community. In Elsfield's case, either Mrs Buchan or Mrs Allam stitched an explanation of the items chosen to represent the village on the back of the banner: the tree because Elsfield stands on a hill and has a lot of elms, which provide shelter for rooks and jackdaws, and the coat of arms of Christ Church because they were and are the landowners. The banner was entered in a competition at the annual fete of the Oxfordshire Federation at New College in the summer of 1921 but there is no record of how it fared, so it seems fair to assume that other banners were better designed and used felt or silk as the main component, rather than sitting-room curtains.

When the branch had got into its stride by 1923 it was providing a very varied range of speakers and topics: talks on home nursing, dress making and cooking, which one might have expected, but also hat making, making sweets and, most surprisingly, demonstrations of soldering and carpentry. As the years passed the variety of speakers available increased. In 1928 there was a talk about care of the hair, including cutting, shingling, bobbing and how to singe long hair, practical gardening, raffia work, a lantern lecture by Miss Hadow about her travels in the far-flung corners of Europe, and a demonstration by Brown & Polson, makers of custard powder. In 1930 they had talks about France, Canada, India and Ceylon, and if they were ever short of ideas there was always Susan Buchan's travels in America to fall back on. Manufacturers of foodstuffs and household gadgets were also keen to mount demonstrations of their products, with Heinz, Brown & Polson, and Sutton's Nurseries eager to show their wares and explain production methods. And if the demonstrators would not come to the branch, the branch would go to them, so visits were arranged to Rowntrees', and Lyons Tea factory.

The branch was also kept in touch with a wider world and its problems by the WI magazine *Home and Country* and by a monthly letter from the National Federation. This was an important way of bringing the issues that needed debating to people in villages that had been at one time remote from the government of the country. In the first half of the twentieth century the rural home was seen as the embodiment of Englishness, where children, seen as a national resource, could be brought up in a healthy environment. This all gave the WI impetus to demand improvements in living conditions, not only in the rural homes of Britain but also for children living abroad. Very early on in the life of the branch, a speaker, Lady Mary Murray, came to talk about the 'Save the Children' fund, which had been set up in 1919 by two sisters, Eglantyne Jebb and Dorothy Buxton, in response to the effect of the trade embargo imposed by the victors of the First World War on the losers. Lady Mary would have told them of the children in Berlin and Vienna whose bones were like rubber because of rickets, of tuberculosis and of children dying of starvation in Armenia. She would have stressed the fact that the children had no clothes, and that hospitals were lacking in practically everything they needed, reduced to using paper to bandage wounds. She touched the hearts of the women of Elsfield, who immediately decided that in view of the 'great distress in Central Europe' they should donate any spare funds they might have to 'Save the Children'.

They were also involved in raising money for projects nearer home. They spent thirty shillings on wool to knit up at their monthly meetings to make money for the Radcliffe Infirmary. In fact, they seem to have followed Madge Watt's lead and knitted their way through every meeting so every moment spent away from home was productive. Many people saved every week so they could afford hospital treatment if they needed it, and the Radcliffe tapped into the resources of the WI when they needed to raise extra money to build an extension. Elsfield was asked to raise £30 (the equivalent of £1,155 today). This was a lot of money for such a small place, but the speaker pointed out that in the previous nine years twenty-six people from Elsfield had been in-patients and fifty-four had attended the hospital as out-patients, so the people of Elsfield had need of the services on offer there. The WI asked for a lady doctor to be appointed.

As Maggie Andrews has written, 'Their new found confidence as skilled workers and their perception of themselves as the heart of the nation were able to be transferred into demands for social welfare legislation.' By the late thirties there were increasingly clear expectations that the state should provide a different level of support for rural communities. By 1937 the women of Elsfield, alongside their colleagues in similar branches throughout the country, were lobbying for cheap milk for expectant mothers and young children, for police to be stationed in every village, for there to be a telephone available, and for analgesics to be provided for women giving birth in rural communities. There were in fact by the late thirties six private telephones in Elsfield – at the manor, the vicarage, three of the four farms and the village telephone, which was installed in the late thirties and which was to prove invaluable to the Home Guard when war broke out, as it was an integral part of the communication system warning the village of impending invasion.

Maggie Andrews asserts that a Housing Act passed in 1919 accepted that it was the state's duty to house a proportion of the working class and that while this was mostly seen in urban terms (a consensus which lasted till the 1980s when Margaret Thatcher encouraged local authorities to sell off council housing), it also affected more rural communities. In response to this the WI accepted responsibility for assessing how many houses a village might need and what repairs were needed. While this may have been the case nationally, there is no evidence that this applied in Elsfield, where the land was owned privately by Christ Church and where everyone in the village apart from the Buchans were living in tied houses. People were in no position to ask for improvements to their cottages, and the village remained without electricity, mains water or sewerage until after the Second World War. The

Buchans had their own generator but Miss Parsons did not, and Mrs Buchan comments on how picturesque the parties for the village children were when lit by lamp and candles at Christmas. Miss Parsons' house was also so cold that you felt as if your feet were freezing to the stone-flagged floor. In spite of that, she lived to be eighty-seven, her health no doubt maintained by a thrice-weekly walk into Oxford, three miles there and three miles back with a steep hill to negotiate, which she continued almost to the end of her life.

One topic that was not touched on either nationally or locally was the question of family planning. This was felt to be too contentious, though in 1930 Lady Denman became a member of the governing body of the Birth Control Council.

The upper echelons of Elsfield society – Miss Parsons, Mrs Buchan, and Mrs Elkington – might have been accused from time to time of cultural imperialism, the middle-class members trying to educate their less-well-educated colleagues. If so, it was more forgivable in Elsfield than in many places. The president was a writer, and the president's husband was a writer of note and a publisher. But Grace Hadow had shown in her talk about poetry to the munitions workers in the First World War that there was a hunger for 'culture', what the people in the big houses enjoyed. Many of the people who heard Grace Hadow speak that evening must have felt they were being excluded from something they would like to know about. This must have been particularly the case in Elsfield, where the manor was visited by all the intelligentsia of the day. Poets galore beat a path to the manor: Walter de la Mare, John Masefield, Sir Henry Newbolt, Robert Graves, the adventurer and writer T. E. Lawrence, Enid Bagnold, author of *National Velvet*, and even Virginia Woolf, herself a member of the

WI and treasurer of her local branch. Politicians too were often to be seen there: Neville Chamberlain, Sir Stafford Cripps, Stanley Baldwin. Education at the village school may have been rather sketchy and a very low priority, especially for the older boys, with the school year fitted round the needs of agriculture, the summer holiday being a moveable feast, lengthened to help with harvest if the corn and barley were late ripening, started early if the crops were ripening early. However, the children were in the habit of learning poetry by heart so they could reach the accepted level of knowledge before they were allowed to leave school. So they were familiar with speeches culled willy-nilly from Shakespeare, they knew Tennyson and Keats, and above all they knew the Bible, read out to them by John Buchan every Sunday in the tiny church, so they were by no means cut off from the finer manifestations of the English language.

It was therefore quite understandable that there should be an immediate response to the Barnett House Library scheme. Mrs Elkington offered to be librarian and members agreed to pay a penny a month subscription. In 1929 they had a literary competition – to write a short story about village life or a poem of eight lines. But what really seems to have grabbed their imagination was amateur dramatics. Here again Barnett House provided a useful source of expertise. Mrs Buchan tactfully suggested that as they were about to embark on putting on plays not only to be performed before doting and not so doting families, but also in front of other branches, it might be a good idea to have someone from Barnett House give them a few guidelines on how to do it. The drama group was established in 1924, and by 1928 they were putting on two plays a year and entering competitions where they were competing against other branches from as far away as Chinnor and Burford.

Not only were they putting on plays themselves, they also organised visits from the Oxfordshire Players, who played to a crowded house, or rather the barn in the manor house yard. Audiences of a hundred were not uncommon, and *The Lord and the Lackey* is recorded by Gentelia Webb, the secretary, as being 'fun and laughter from beginning to end'. Occasionally the Buchan children used the WI as an audience for their play writing, acting and reciting, Master Alastair Buchan performing three recitations in April 1929 while his sister Alice gave a short talk on the Women's Institutes in England and Scotland, followed by a recitation. Mrs Buchan's offer to give readings from Dickens was one bit of cultural imperialism that was firmly resisted by the members. When she offered to read from *Pickwick Papers* it was turned down in favour of a talk on 'What to do till the doctor comes'.

If treading the boards was not your thing, then the drama subcommittee would organise singing, which everyone could join in with, sending for song sheets from the *Oxford Times* and performing folk songs at the annual exhibition organised by the Oxfordshire Federation of WIs at New College. Or you could attend a lecture by Grace Hadow herself on 'Old Customs' or 'The words we use', which was 'so entertaining and carefully explained that one was sorry when so interesting a lecture came to an end'. Or there was Margaret Deneke talking about her work with Dr Arnold Schweitzer at his medical mission in Africa, or a little later, in 1933, a talk by Miss Doris Aldridge entitled 'The Secrets of Broadcasting'. The BBC had begun making programmes specifically for the WI in 1930, and Mrs Elkington had asked anyone in the village with a wireless to ask neighbours in to listen. Suddenly the village was alive and buzzing with activity, alert to what was happening not just in Oxford, but in a wider world. They could find out what life was like in Albania and Ceylon, Africa and the Balkans. They even had a talk about Geneva from 'a lady who has been there'.

One of Madge Watt's comments was that if you wanted to attract young members you had to make the WI fun, though not frivolous. Elsfield entered into the swing of it with enthusiasm, with fetes, parties and trips away from the village. The invention of the motor car, and its bigger cousins, the omnibus and the charabanc, made travel easy and meant that a day trip to the seaside or to London was perfectly feasible. Gone were trips in the carrier's cart to Oxford squashed in alongside packages, parcels and sacks. In came the bus with a regular service to Oxford, and charabanc outings to Bournemouth cost eleven shillings, collected in weekly instalments by Miss Parsons, or one could travel to Bognor or Windsor. They were long days and not for the faint-hearted. You had to be up, breakfasted and dressed – corsets laced, stockings suspended, hat firmly in place – and waiting outside Tree Cottage by seven o'clock, and you would not be back until late evening. Only women with compliant husbands could embark on these trips, which may be why Mrs Hambidge could only assemble fourteen people for a trip to Malvern when twenty-four people were needed to fill the charabanc. The spa town, with its links to the composer Elgar, obviously had less appeal than the more glamorous Windsor with its links to royalty, or Bournemouth, and you couldn't paddle at Malvern, either.

The parties they organised, not just for themselves but for the men and children of the village, must have been enormous fun, though strictly speaking they may not have fitted the 'no frivolity' specified by Madge Watt. What would she have thought about

Susan Buchan's suggestion that they should try eating jelly with skewers, or Mrs Clinkard's idea of seeing how many biscuits you could eat in a given time? Though 'Sing, say, play or pay' might have met with her approval, played at the picnic in Miss Parsons' garden. The fete, held in the grounds of the manor, soon became an established event which raised substantial amounts of money for the church and welcomed people from the surrounding villages. There was bowling for a pig, won in 1923 by Mr Tom Newell and Miss Bowerman. Mr Newell's prize was the pig and Miss Bowerman's was a tea service. There was also 'Striking the ham blindfold', won by Mr Blowing, and a treasure hunt whose winner failed to collect the prize. There was dancing to the music of Mr Haynes and his band, and a concert in the evening given by Climo and his troupe. A packed day that entailed a lot of organisation but was well worth the effort.

In 1935 Elsfield WI suffered a serious blow to its social life and its morale when John Buchan was raised to the peerage as Lord Tweedsmuir of Elsfield prior to taking up his position as Governor-General of Canada. Susan Buchan, or Lady Tweedsmuir as she now was, resigned in July of that year in preparation for leaving for Canada. The Tweedsmuirs left Euston on 25 October, bound for Liverpool, seen off at the station by their daughter Alice, her husband, and their second son William, and accompanied by ladies-in-waiting, one of whom, Beatrice Spencer-Smith, wrote to her mother that Susie cried most of the way to Crewe and her husband did nothing to console her. Besides the distress she must have felt in leaving three of her children in England – Johnny was in Uganda suffering from amoebic dysentery – one of the factors in her distress must have been the loss of so many friendships she had made in Elsfield and the county WI. She would be sadly missed in Elsfield. Mrs Clinkard had expressed the feelings of the branch when she thanked Lady Tweedsmuir for all her kindnesses over the last fifteen years and gave their best wishes for her future in Canada.

Miss Deneke was elected president and moved to centre stage as she tried to emulate Susan Buchan's generosity. She arranged an outing to Oxford University Press with tea afterwards at Lady Margaret Hall. Susan Tweedsmuir kept in touch with the branch by cables, which were read out at the meetings, and suggested that they should correspond with a Canadian WI, an idea which was followed up. John Buchan died in 1940 and his ashes are buried in Elsfield churchyard, but his wife was not able to come home immediately because of the difficulty of travelling by sea across the Atlantic with the threat of U-boat attacks. When she did, she immediately threw herself into the war work for which the WI is famous.

In 1937 Lady Denman summed up the progress the WI had made since its formation. 'To my mind' she said in a broadcast, 'the greatest achievement of the Institutes is that we have learned to govern ourselves. We do not believe in dictators; we believe that each member should be responsible for her Institute and should have a share of the work.' This at a time when Germany, Italy and Russia were ruled by dictators and Spain was soon to follow.

6

'WE WOMEN HATE WAR': THE WAR
YEARS, 1939–1945

Delegates to the 1939 AGM got a taste of what might be to come when Madge Watt, who was about to retire from the executive of the Associated Countrywomen of the World, introduced speakers from various countries around the world. They each gave a short address in their own language, but when the German representative, who was very warmly received, had finished speaking, she gave a Nazi salute, while the Italian gave a similar fascist salute. What, I wonder, were the thoughts flashing through Grace Hadow's mind, or Lady Denman's? Whatever their private thoughts on the matter, Lady Denman went on to speak about rural water supplies and anaesthesia for countrywomen when giving birth. The delegate from the Langley branch, in Berkshire, commented that there were a lot of speeches about childcare, most of them much too long!

Much has been written about the war years but one of the most direct works is *Mrs Milburn's Diaries*, because it was written at the time it all happened, though not published till much later. Mrs Milburn lived in Burleigh, a village near Coventry. She was a member of her local WI, maintaining their notice board and being an enthusiastic member of their drama group. She takes us through the bombing of Coventry, rationing and work with evacuees, and she epitomises the spirit of 'Keep Calm and Carry On'. As well as working for the WI she also worked for the WVS, took part in the Voluntary Car Transport scheme and sewed for the Red Cross. When her only child, Alan, was taken prisoner at Dunkirk, she participated in a POW support group for relatives of prisoners of war, which provided information for families about such things as living conditions and what prisoners needed. She sent regular parcels to Alan, writing to him twice a week. A surprising number of letters got through to Alan and came back from him. He recounted how he was putting on weight, had bought a Rolex watch, was gardening and had been to the cinema. Nevertheless, once her initial anxiety to know whether he was alive, and what the extent of his injuries were, had been assuaged, she commented each Christmas and on his birthday on how long the war was going on, and how much she missed him.

She was a staunch Conservative, and made disparaging remarks about any Labour minister who dared challenge any of Churchill's decisions. On her husband Jack's birthday in 1941 she bought him a Union Jack, which they duly hoisted at various times when battles were going well. She keeps us abreast of the news from the war zone as reported on the BBC. She gives a vivid picture of what day-to-day life was like, giving the price of foodstuffs, describing how little there was in the shop windows, and giving details of how her garden was progressing.

She had a maid, Kate, who had stayed with them for forty-seven years, and a gardener, who retired during the course of the war. Her husband Jack had also retired. What puzzled me at first was the amount of time they spent in bed if they had a cold. They took to their beds for several days, and the doctor was often in attendance at a cost of seven shillings and sixpence a visit. Then I remembered that there were no antibiotics then, and colds could soon develop into pneumonia, which was a killer. Mrs Milburn records her anxiety about Churchill, who 'has a patch on his lung' following a bout of flu. Her own colds were treated with a bottle of medicine from the doctor, which was sent with the milk the day after a visit.

In the first week of September, 1939, she describes fitting blackout curtains. By 2 September 'the blackout was already done – we'd gone into Leamington the week before to buy blackout curtain material, and when they said "How much do you want? There are twenty six yards in this roll" I said I'd take the lot.' It was not enough, however.

> During the week we were called up by the air raid warden, who found our blackout insufficient and still more curtains had to be made. By now the price of the material had gone up from two shillings and sixpence to three shillings and eleven pence a yard, and the quality was decidedly inferior. But a very definite blackout was obtained at the bay windows by covering the whole bay from the top of the pelmet to a foot from the floor, with a great black pall reminiscent of a first-class French funeral.

At government level, preparations had been in place long before war was declared. In the spring of 1938 the Ministry of Agriculture turned its attention to how they would manage the land resources and who would work the land in the event of war. The permanent secretary decided to set up a women's branch of the ministry and asked Lady Denman to head it. The government also wanted a list of people suitable to occupy one or two subordinate posts and to set up women's county committees. Trudie consulted the national executive of the WI about this, as this new post, if she took it, would impact on her capacity to carry on as chairman of the WI. The executive was adamant that she should take on this new responsibility. With her experience of the Land Army in the First World War she was the obvious person to do the job. She would also be able to use her knowledge of the women out in the county federations who would be prepared to set up county committees.

Using the WI lists of members, Trudie worked with Frances Farrer, the national executive's general secretary, and wrote to the people she thought best suited to fill the posts. Lady Denman was convinced of the importance of her work, as during the First World War the country had had only three weeks' supply of food left when the harvest failed in 1917. She was determined this would not happen if she could help it. 'The Land Army fights in the fields. It is in the fields of Britain that the most critical battle of the war may well be fought and won,' she declared in 1939. The Women's Land Army (WLA) was formed on 1 June 1939 and two groups of land girls were trained and ready for work by the time war was declared in September 1939.

The administrative headquarters were set up at Balcombe Place, Lady Denman's home, five days before war began. There were fourteen officers and thirty-five clerks and typists, mostly from the Ministry of Agriculture. There was also a chief administrative officer, to be responsible for finance and correspondence with government departments. The people who were working there had a very pleasant time. When they arrived at Balcombe Place at the beginning of their time there, they were driven from the station to the house in a fleet of cars including Trudie's Rolls-Royce. They were given the freedom of the place. There was the swimming pool, and tennis and hockey were arranged for them. Indoors there was a gramophone for dancing, table tennis and darts. Their bedrooms were delightful, kitted out with electric kettles for tea-making, and if they were out late milk and biscuits were left out for them. Trudie was unstinting in her generosity. All she insisted on was punctuality at meal times. She often joined the staff in games of table tennis, darts and other games. Lord Denman left Balcombe House for the duration of the war and lived in a hotel in Hove, where he subsequently set up house, though he came back to Balcombe House occasionally on a Sunday.

Lady Denman used up a fair amount of petrol in the course of her work, and petrol rations were limited to enough fuel for 1,800 miles a year, though extra coupons were allowed for war work. When she was refused extra petrol for her very small car she had to threaten to give up her work for the WI if the extra coupons were not forthcoming. She wrote directly to Lord Woolton, Minister of Food: 'If I have to resign because I cannot get petrol, the Institutes will draw the conclusion that the Government does not place any value on their national efforts. Institute members are well aware of the allowances made to other organisations' (i.e. the Women's Voluntary Service and the WLA). The petrol coupons were immediately made available to her so she could carry on her visits. There was, needless to say, a great deal of bureaucracy to contend with if you did have access to extra petrol. Mrs Milburn writes on 1 February, 1944,

The morning's work, after the usual duties, was to fill in FORMS and records of journeys for the Women's Land Army and the Volunteer Car Pool. Twenty-four forms and two records for the former, detailing every girl and every journey. The Volunteer Car Pool records I fill in after every journey, but still they must be set down again on a summary sheet, and on the back there are a, b, c, d, e, f, g, h, and i to be filled in and half-way down the page 'the two totals must be the same', and again at the bottom of the page. And sometimes I just can't do the sums and, signing my name at the foot and telling the Volunteer Car Pool officer how much petrol I have got left, leave her to fill it in.

There was a considerable overlap of personnel between the WLA and the WI. Not that older ladies of the WI went out and dug the land or harvested potatoes, but the land girls needed some sort of supervision and encouragement. They also needed someone who could speak up for them if there were difficulties and someone who would act as mediator between them and the farmers they worked for. Mrs Milburn in Warwickshire was one such. She regularly did the rounds, visiting her allotted 'girls' and trying to provide them with home comforts and something other than work in their lives. The girls often lived in hostels, and in June 1944 she writes, 'Tonight nine land-girls came, did a quiz and were very merry. They ate up all the buns and cakes and drank many cups of tea.' In Wiltshire the Hon. Mrs Anthony Methuen was county chairman for the WLA. She had been on the executive of the NFWI, thirteen years as treasurer and a trustee until her death in 1972. Her daughter, Lady Elizabeth Fraser, describes the work she did at the time. 'She had the responsibility of the girls, making sure they were living in decent conditions and, if they were ill, to see that they were looked after.' She then continues in a language that would be thought completely unacceptable today – she was writing in the 1980s so we must excuse it – 'Then there were the naughty girls who got themselves in the family way.' (As my own daughter points out to me, it takes two!) 'Mummy used to have to go and talk to them quietly and look after them ... A lot of the girls coming from towns found it very difficult to adjust, and this is where my mother came in.'

At the same time as the Ministry of Agriculture was contacting Lady Denman in 1938, the Home Secretary sent for the Marchioness of Reading and asked her to set up a Women's Voluntary Service whose role would be in the event of war to organise evacuees and run canteens and other services to support victims of enemy action. She formed a committee of representatives from various women's organisations, but this did not include the WI, though they were asked to suggest suitable candidates who could be recruited from the WI into the ranks of the WVS, a suggestion which did not go down well and was not implemented. The NFWI in its turn referred to its original constitution, which stated that no institution should participate in discussions or actions that might infringe on the religious beliefs of other members. As a number of Quakers were members of the WI and they were pacifists, the NFWI decided that while individual members were free to act in any way they thought appropriate, branches could not take part in overt war work. The national executive issued a statement saying that while the institutes could give valuable help by arranging hospitality for evacuated mothers and children and by helping with home safety, it was not appropriate for them to become involved with Air Raid Precautions, because this was the responsibility of the local authorities and could be performed by both men and women equally.

Lady Denman knew that one of the many important jobs a branch could do was to maintain the morale of village people.

She wrote, 'We feel it to be of greatest importance that Women's Institutes' monthly meetings should maintain their educational and social character, thus providing for the members a centre of tranquillity and cheerfulness in a sadly troubled world.' Lady Tweedsmuir wrote from Canada in similar vein, though rather more graphically, to the women of Elsfield. 'Do continue the meetings', she said, 'even if you have to drink water and gnaw on a carrot!' The women of Elsfield took her at her word, but each brought a pinch of tea with them to make 'the Elsfield blend'.

Mrs Milburn's WI put on a play, *Hide and Seek*, in 1942. 'If only the performers would learn their parts we might get on,' she comments acerbically, 'but everyone's life is so full these days.' They also had fancy-dress parties, at one of which, at the beginning of 1941, dressed as Old Mother Hubbard in an old green skirt, a figured blouse, mob cap, white stockings and new bedroom slippers, she won a prize for the prettiest costume. This was only a couple of months after the terrible bombing of Coventry when refugees had flooded out of the city into the surrounding villages. Two years later she was doing the same thing again. 'I thought what a silly old party I am,' she says, 'And next, how can we waste even a few hours on these childish things? And then how little relaxation one gets on the whole, so perhaps it is a good thing.' In the summer of 1940 she was busy preparing a charade for the WI to represent National Savings, with Britannia holding the baby called National Savings, talking to various people who came to see it. The drama group came round to rehearse it in the afternoon and she finished off the day with a trip round the village delivering WI notices. The following week she had intended to go to the cinema to see *Gone with the Wind*, but 'in last night's raid the cinema was demolished'.

The Food Supply

In July 1938, a month after the NFWI had issued their statement about what was appropriate action for WI members, the Prime Minister, Neville Chamberlain, gave a speech to farmers in Kettering in which he said there was 'no need to encourage the greatest output of food at home because ample supplies would continue from overseas in the event of war'. At this time less than 10 per cent of the onions used in Britain were grown here, and less than half the carrots. Secretly, however, as early as 1933, plans had already been made to control prices, wages and profits in the event of a major war. The government was building on experiences gained in the second half of the First World War, and their aims were two-fold: to increase the fertility of the land by maintaining livestock production, and to plough up grassland immediately war was declared, so that the supply of human and animal foodstuffs could be increased very rapidly. It was also proposed that War Emergency Committees be set up to oversee wartime needs. Local people had been selected to run these committees, though they were not aware of it at the time.

In 1936, therefore, grants had become available to farmers for drainage, and subsidies were introduced for fertiliser, which led in the war years to a doubling of the quantity of potash and phosphate applied to the fields. A wheat subsidy that was already in place had been extended to barley and oats. By 1939 there was also a payment of £2 an acre for every acre ploughed up between May and September 1939. The aim was to have 2 million acres of grassland ploughed in time for the 1940 harvest.

Rationing

Before the war, Britain imported enormous amounts of food: 20 million tons shipped from the four corners of the world. The enemy strategy was therefore to blockade the ships bringing food to Britain with the aim of starving the country into submission.

Rationing was introduced early in 1940. Food, petrol, clothing, soap and paper were all rationed at one time or another between 1939 and 1948. In fact, bread was not rationed until after the war had ended, because of the terrible weather in 1946 which resulted in poor harvests. The system was intended to be egalitarian and it succeeded in that aim, with the population healthier and infant mortality reduced because of the careful sharing out of resources. Mrs Milburn records their last unrationed meal of the war on 10 March 1940. While there seemed to be plenty of food in the early days, as the war went on rations became very tight. Mrs Milburn wrote about the joint she got at the butcher's in October 1943, 'Well, it very nearly would have gone through the hole in a tram ticket.'

People registered with a grocer, a butcher and a milkman. They were allowed one egg a week or a packet of dried egg a month, and three pints of milk a week, though more for children and pregnant women. The first items to be rationed were bacon, butter and sugar, followed by meat, though sausages and offal were only rationed between 1942 and 1944. The meat content in sausages was very small and the bulk was made up of bread. Tea, margarine and cooking fats followed, with preserves and cheese added in 1941. There was no variety of cheese. Children growing up during the war did not know there were different kinds. Cheese was 'Mousetrap', and that was that.

Mrs Milburn also comments in October 1939 how busy the roads were, with convoys of trucks, vans, aeroplane carriers, ambulances and, from time to time, lorries full of troops. By July 1940 she was recording that the roads had become very quiet.

No longer is the road crowded with pleasure cars, business vans and vehicles, but the long empty road stretches for half a mile or so, often with nothing to be seen on it at all. In the evening the village is quiet, with scarcely a soul to be seen walking about. But it is not a happy tranquillity. It is unnatural and eerie, and tense at times. Behind it lies the unhappiness and anxiety of war and not knowing what will happen to our dear, dear, land in the next few months.

Much of women's time was spent queuing, and some items, such as cigarettes, were kept under the counter. Mrs Milburn records that she spent twenty minutes in the food counsellor's office getting a permit for butter and sugar for the Women's Institute teas. Individuals had ration books, which had to be taken to the shops every time you went shopping. In 1943 Mrs Milburn lost her ration book. 'I knew it must be in the house or the garden,' she says, 'but had to get my rations today without it when I went on my bicycle to the grocer. Such a heavy basket, it made the bike wobble a bit. This evening, when getting the cushions out of the oak chest for the land-girls to sit on in the garden, there, deep down in the chest was my ration book.' Of course, food was available outside the rationing system. Mrs Milburn records bartering apples and pears, of which she had a great many, for a cockerel. And there was the black market, which Mrs Milburn does not mention. Besides being illegal, it was also considered unpatriotic, so she probably didn't make use of it, though many people did.

Food Production

Food production became a major concern. A Produce Guild was set up by the WI. It was run on county lines and there were two sections, a food production section and a 'use and preservation of produce' section. The aim was for every village to become self-supporting in vegetables and to run pig clubs. The WI carried on with competitions for who could produce the best of a variety of products. In Berkswell, Mrs Milburn's branch, the produce exhibition was held in the institute, and she found the judges in the thick of judging the merits of jams, jellies, chutneys, salad cream and bottled fruit. 'Mrs Ford was sipping each bottle of wine and looking flushed by the time she got to the eleventh,' she writes.

The slogan 'Dig for Victory' advertised the idea of food production as one of the many ways to support the war effort. Vegetable production was seen as especially capable of improvement given that so many of the vegetables eaten at that time came from abroad. Large quantities of onions had been imported from France and Spain before the war, but now these were not available. The onion harvest of 1941 was awaited eagerly. Unfortunately there had been bad weather in August so the growth was poor, and those onions that did grow would not keep well. Onions did rather better the following year, but they were nothing like as good as the pre-war foreign imports. Now we have onions that will grow more quickly and make good use of what daylight is available. In the 1940s onions needed a long growing season and could not cope with the cold, the wet and the dark in the early months of the year in Britain. Mrs Milburn's onions were all infested with onion fly, and she had trouble with wireworms. She named them as she dug them up – Himmler, Goebbels, Goering, and stamped on each one.

Other crops did rather better. Potatoes, of course, were grown not only by individuals, but by farmers in the fields where in the past they had grazed sheep. In Elsfield, the land, which had for many years been used for grazing sheep because of the light soil, was turned over to potatoes for feeding the army.

At the time of Dunkirk, Trudie was asked by the government to broadcast to the Women's Institutes throughout Britain. In her talk she said, 'I have been lucky enough to work with countrywomen for many years and I know their pluck, I know their resourcefulness and I know their good sense. These great qualities are just what are wanted now.' Later that summer she sent out a letter to the institutes emphasising the importance of their role in helping to safeguard the nation's food.

It was acknowledged that people working in some kinds of manual labour needed extra food to keep them working efficiently. Canteens and British restaurants could provide meals extra to rationing for people working in factories, but for farm workers, who often took their food into the fields with them, there was nothing. The Rural Pie Scheme was developed to counter this imbalance and the pies were distributed in small towns by the WVS, who were unable, however, to cover the more remote areas, where distribution was undertaken by the WI. The pies were made by local bakers, and in Elsfield Mrs Phipps became secretary of the WI Produce Guild and also agreed to distribute the pies, which cost four pence. She did this for four and a half years. Betty Houghton, in Chiddingly in Sussex, who joined the WI when she was sixteen, was the pie distributor for her locality. 'They looked a bit like Cornish pasties,' she said. 'The art was deciding how many to order each week so we didn't run out or have a lot left over.' Hilary Morris's research into the pie scheme in Cheshire has shown that nearly a million pies were sold in Cheshire in 1944 alone. Perhaps best not to enquire what went into the pies! The meat ration for cafés, canteens and restaurants was one pennyworth per person per meal – about an ounce in each pie. The rest would have been vegetables, especially potatoes, which were used in everything, including bread, to stop people feeling hungry.

Vegetable gardens became even more important than before the war. Many people had pigsties in the garden and pig clubs were encouraged. Farmers were allowed to keep pigs but the slaughter was carefully controlled. A slaughter licence had to be applied for in person and the resulting carcass took three hard days' work to process. First the pig was cut up into joints, then bacon and hams were salted and black pudding made from the blood. Lard was made from the fat and the intestines were washed to be used for sausage skins. The bladder could be used as a football.

Nationally people were encouraged to breed rabbits, not only for the meat but for the fur, which could be used to make gloves and hats. In 1944 Mrs Churchill organised a 'Fur for Russia' scheme. Under this scheme, which was in operation for two and a half years, coats, waistcoats, hoods and caps were lined with rabbit fur and sent to Russia. As well as protecting people against the bitter cold of a Russian winter, it was a way of building sympathy for the Russian people, who were now our allies. Gardening books of the period offered advice on how to set up both poultry and rabbit runs, though they say nothing about how to control the rats, which often accompany such activities. *Practical Gardening and Food Production in Pictures* reprinted in 1946 suggests that one buck and four does would be enough to keep a family of four in rabbit meat for one day a week. The skins should be carefully removed and dried by nailing them on to boards before they were sent to a reliable firm for dressing. Mrs Roberts of Trefnant WI in Denbighshire received a handwritten latter from Mrs Churchill thanking her for the pelts she sent, and Ely reported that their appeal for rabbit skins had resulted in fifty-four rabbit skins, though they asked that the skins be properly dried before they were sent. The editor of *Home and Country* commented that 'The arrival of a moist and unpleasant parcel of rabbit skins had a most unpleasant effect upon the County Secretary of Derby.'

As soon as war broke out in September 1939 Miss Farrer, the NFWI general secretary, contacted the Ministry of Food and obtained 430 tons of sugar. She then wrote to county chairmen telling them what she had done, and explaining that the sugar was for preserving; the minimum quantity supplied to them would be one hundredweight (fifty kilos) costing £1 7s 6d. At first the preserving was done on an ad hoc basis, but in 1940 the first jamming and fruit preservation centres were set up. They were organised as a way of channelling precious sugar out to people and to control the supply so individuals could not siphon it off for private use or sell on the black market. Preserving centres had to be open to everyone in the community, not just WI members, and must be run co-operatively. Official log books were sold (five shillings each) to record what had been jammed and canned. There were strict rules about what the sugar could be used for. The sugar, which had to be ordered through the county federation, had to be applied for and the permit was valid only for two months. It had to be used for jams, jellies, fruit cheeses, chutneys, fruit juices and canned or bottled fruit. It could not be used for marmalade, mincemeat, homemade wines, cider or perry. Strawberries, blackcurrants and raspberries were only to be used for jams, not for canning. Cans went to hospitals, army camps and public canteens while anything which did not pass the rigorous tests applied by the inspectors was sent to schools! In 1940, 1,170 tons of fruit was saved nationally, which would otherwise have rotted. Some 2,600 village centres registered for jamming or canning.

The work involved in setting up and running these centres was immense, as letters to and from the Oxfordshire County Federation show. Helena Deneke was the honorary secretary of the federation, and Miss Ashcroft was president. Between them they wrote to the many branches in the county asking if they would set up a preserving centre. The replies show just how stressed people were because of the war, the sheer difficulties of getting around the county, and how difficult it was to communicate with the men in suits in Whitehall who had little day-to-day knowledge of horticulture. Members in Ambrosden, who had been asked to join Islip centre, said they couldn't get there because of the lack of a bus service. They could, however, get their plums to Blackthorne or Arncott. Could they do that? Miss Ashworth said they could but they must keep accurate records of the fruit they took and the jam they made. Letters to Miss Deneke and Miss Ashcroft show the personal difficulties some women were enduring. May E. H. replies from Kelmscott to Miss Deneke, a personal friend whom she addresses as 'My dear Lena':

> Much as I would like to agree to have a preserving depot here I feel I can't say yes. I really have a great deal to do here what with evacuees and my husband's writing and tabulating for his survey of all the farms under his control. I hate refusing but you will see how it is. I find that I get awfully tired now with too much work and I have to do a lot in the garden among the vegetables.

Hook Norton was in difficulties, too. Eleanor Ball writes,

> I am sorry to trouble you but I think you know of my eldest sister's serious illness. My other sister broke down and has had to go away for rest. They being respectively President and Secretary of the WI, this has caused no little confusion, particularly over jam-making.

There was a complaint about the quality of the produce. The grocer Grimbly Hughes of Oxford, who was collecting the jars of jam, complained that some of the jars were sticky and that one had gone mouldy. Grimbly Hughes offered to buy the jam at reduced cost because they thought they could sell it to the soldiers' canteen.

At one centre, the secretary resigned because of the enormous amount of work involved, at another the supervisor refused to supervise because she was booked up and had no spare time in her work schedule. The secretary, Miss Dickens, whose sister had just had a stroke, wrote decisively to say that she had closed the centre. It was not, in her opinion, a suitable place anyway, because there was no water in the hall. Ipsden gave the sugar to people in their own homes, which was expressly forbidden by Whitehall, and there was a plaintive query from one branch who asked how they were supposed to organise the jam making when the fruit ripened in August, September and October, and the sugar came in one job lot. Dorchester had an enthusiastic band of jammers, but no sugar, and they filled in the forms wrongly. Charlbury labelled their red plums blue plums and overcooked the fruit for bottling, while the lady whose house was used as a centre in Headington had forgotten to have her gas meter read before the preserving started, so did not have an accurate record of gas consumption. Elsfield, however, being a very small place, cut through much of the red tape. The preserving centre was at Miss Parsons' house and she didn't charge for the fuel. Lady Tweedsmuir at the manor, having returned from Canada on the death of her husband, advanced the money for the sugar and bottles upfront and Mrs Aste, the new vicar's wife, sold the jam to villagers at cost price, so they made no profit. The supervisor, Mrs Marshall, cycled up to Elsfield so there were no travel expenses and the cooking utensils were lent by Miss Parsons, Mrs Aste and Lady Tweedsmuir. By 11 October 1940 they had made 1,200 pounds of jam and bottled 380 bottles of fruit. Please could they do the same next year, they asked the county organiser, their very own Helena Deneke?

Elsfield was unusual in that it had two relatively wealthy women who were prepared to subsidise the process, but it is not surprising, given the red tape and the stress caused by the difficult circumstances, that the 4,500 centres set up in 1941 had fallen to 3,366 by May 1943. Viola Williams was one of the WI inspectors who checked the quality of the produce. She stresses the honesty of these jam-making centres. The sugar was given on trust but, as Viola points out, because there had to be 60 per cent sugar content in every batch of jam made, it was easy to calculate whether any had gone missing. Viola also had to check for cleanliness, packaging, and labelling. In her book *Jambusters*, Julie Summers considers that the jam-making of 1939, which was so efficiently and speedily carried out, showed how the WI could swing into effective action and convinced the government, and in particular Lord Woolton, appointed Minister of Food in 1940, that it was an organisation which could prove its worth in the coming struggle. He wrote to Lady Denman at the end of 1940, 'This was work of national importance demanding administrative ability of a high order at the Headquarters of your organisation and local initiative and cooperation which are a fine example of democratic action at its best.'

Canning centres worked in the same way. Canning machines could be borrowed from county organisations or were sometimes sent from Canada or America. Four mobile canning vans were sent by the American Business and Professional Women's Federation, and proved their worth. Studley Priory, in Oxfordshire, borrowed a canning machine from Barnett House for two shillings and sixpence and its members were delighted with the result. The mobile vans did not produce easy working conditions, however. As Cicely McCall writes in *Women's Institutes*, 'If you like dripping heat, cramped space and perspiring companions, then the inside of a canning van is just the place for you!' The machines needed a high level of skill to operate them. There were several processes involved: sterilisation, grading, packing, making syrup and labelling. Everyone involved had to have passed a test to ensure a reasonable level of competence, and the cans were inspected by the NFWI. Canning machines were available through the Ministry of Agriculture, while the cans could be had from the Metal Box Company. They were allowed to can fruit and tomatoes and later vegetables, which were trickier, according to Viola Williams, a demonstrator for the Produce Guild, because they had to be cooked in a pressure cooker.

Margaret Leech, another instructor, remembers the difficulty she sometimes had in rural areas because of the lack of running water. The cans had to be filled with fruit and syrup then boiled and cooled very quickly, for which you needed cold water. 'You got used to not having a sink,' she says. 'Very often you had to take them outside in a net and cool them under the pump.' On one occasion she asked where the pump was and was told 'It's in the brook'. The brook was in a little ravine so Margaret had to slither down the bank with a net full of very hot cans. Not the easiest of working conditions!

The Produce Guild held lectures and practical demonstrations on all kinds of agricultural practices. Viola Williams was one of a team of lecturers who toured the country with a caravan. There were four of them, known as 'the Circus'. There was a poultry woman, a dairy produce specialist, a home economics lecturer and Viola herself, a horticulturalist. Viola tells how she travelled throughout the length and breadth of Britain, driving along quiet roads with a book in one hand to while away the time, one eye on the book and the other on the road!

Seed distribution was rigidly controlled. The NFWI distributed seeds supplied by Sutton's, which were available at a reduced price if ordered in advance. They were sent out to local branches to distribute. Again, this was a task which fell to Mrs Milburn, except that she was ill in bed so her husband Jack and maid Kate took the job on. During the course of the war 140,000 fruit bushes and 134,000 packets of seeds sent from America and Canada were sold to members of the Produce Guild. In Elsfield, late on in the war when Lady Tweedsmuir had returned to England, seeds were sent from Canada and distributed by Lady Tweedsmuir herself.

On the health front, the WI distributed cod-liver oil and rosehip syrup for children and ensured the distribution of information about the necessity of immunisation against diphtheria and the prevention of sexually transmitted diseases. Because of the lack of citrus fruits such as oranges and lemons, the government was concerned that children might be lacking in Vitamin C. They therefore asked the WI and other voluntary bodies to collect rosehips, which are rich in the vitamin but cannot be eaten in their raw state. A pound of rosehips provides as much Vitamin C as twelve large oranges, so the rosehips were sent to manufacturers who processed them into rosehip syrup. In 1945 Elizabeth Hess, in an article in *Home and Country*, appealed to people to carry on collecting the hips because syrup was still needed for children abroad. 'Recently,' she wrote, '1000 gallons of the syrup were flown to France for Polish children living in a war camp under appalling conditions, where they had been assembled by the Germans to harvest root vegetables.' The WI also collected herbs such as foxglove (which produces digoxin for treating heart disease) to help in the production of drugs.

Make Do and Mend

Many WI branches had speakers on the subject of what would now be called recycling. In Elsfield a Mrs Kreyer gave a talk on salvage. Bones could be made into fat, glue and manure, she said. As the war went on, bones became scarcer, however, because dogs were being fed on scraps. Bones, ash and swill were kept separately, and all paper was saved for re-manufacture. Mrs Milburn was cross because there were bins outside her house which were not being cleared regularly.

I came home and spoke very forcibly on the telephone to the assistant surveyor about moving the wastepaper bin from the verge in front of the house. I reminded him that last 1 April, after my complaint, a letter came saying they would remove it at once. Nothing was done. A further reply came at the beginning of July, after a second complaint, and later I spoke to him on the telephone.

He now promises to come and see for himself on Monday. They cleared the paper out of the bins on Thursday, but the tins which people will pile outside are now augmented by a child's rusty motorcar, bottles and jam jars. It is really too much. And he said then: "Of course you know there's a war on."

An article in *Home and Country* showed that an envelope could be made into fifty cartridge wads, one broken fork and an old bucket made a Tommy Gun, while one ton of mixed rags could be recycled into 250 battledresses and thirteen army tents. It also pointed out that every pound of bones could be rendered down to produce two ounces of glycerine, which makes double its weight of Nitro-glycerine.

Mrs Julyan describes how she came to speak on the subject of 'make do and mend'. 'I had been a domestic science teacher,' she explained, 'and the branch was short of speakers so decided to ask members to give a talk on any area of expertise they felt they had.' Mrs Julyan couldn't do a cookery demonstration because there was nothing to cook and there were no facilities, but she could do dress-making, except that there was no material available. The only thing they had was clothes they already possessed, so she was pushed willy-nilly into thinking up ideas about how to adapt what was available. People learned how to make felt slippers from old felt hats, rugs from old stockings and rags, not to mention blouses out of old dresses. In one village the WI were called on to adapt the Queen Alexandra nursing outfits, which consisted of men's khaki combat trousers and jacket stiff with the chemicals used to kill vermin, into reasonable uniforms, which they duly did.

Knitting for the armed forces was also something which the WI could do. The wool was supplied for this by the government and old jumpers would be unravelled and the wool washed to straighten it before being re-knitted. It was a relief to many branches towards the end of the war to have pink wool to knit children's clothes for the stricken communities in liberated countries such as Greece and Holland instead of the khaki and blue they had knitted for the previous five years.

Evacuees

Maggie Andrews writes that evacuation was 'one of the administrative messes of all time'. She may well be right. In September 1938 Neville Chamberlain, along with French and Italian delegations, went to Munich to parley with Hitler over the future of the parts of Czechoslovakia known as Sudetenland that bordered on Germany. Germany wanted to annex it because there were a great many German speakers and also because there was a lot of heavy industry which would be useful to them. There was panic at Whitehall that if he failed to reach an agreement with the Führer, bombing would start immediately. Arranging the evacuation of vulnerable people from areas likely to be bombed was a task allotted to the WVS, but in the event that organisation was not sufficiently organised to do the job when the need arose and the task was taken up by the WI. On Saturday 24 September 1938 Frances Farrar, secretary of the NFWI, was summoned to Lady Reading's office and told of the government's urgent instructions to put plans into action for the evacuation of vulnerable people. If the Prime Minister and the Führer did not reach agreement about the Sudetenland, the country would be at war within a week. The plan was for the WVS to appoint liaison officers in every county due to receive evacuees. These officers would organise everything at the local level, but while they managed to put liaison officers in place, the rest of the WVS infrastructure was not robust enough to carry out the task. The Home Office suddenly realised that while they had planned for school children to leave, they had no plans to evacuate children under five whose mothers could not leave London. What should they do, and more to the point, what could the WI do?

Step forward Frances Farrer, secretary to the national executive, and other members of the National Federation, who immediately wrote to every county federation in the evacuation area. Frances then sent her 'flying squad' of six VCOs to visit every liaison officer in the area. Miss Farrer was renowned for her administrative ability and her calmness in the face of panic. She had four days to organise something so every moment was precious, she wrote.

> On the night of the twenty-seventh we wrote to 218 welfare centres in the London area ... We had an instantaneous and overwhelming response ... The mothers were pathetically anxious to have their younger children transferred. By Wednesday night, the twenty-eight, we had applications on behalf of 7,000 children.

She went on,

> We were able to obtain the permission of the Matron of St Thomas's Hospital to recruit escorts from the Massage Department students. Sixty volunteers thus became available at once. Other escorts were recruited through the clinics and through Women's Voluntary Services ... The London Transport Board offered us a hundred of their Greenline buses. Women's Voluntary Services had a panel of

cars and were prepared to call up many of their volunteers ... By Wednesday we had a fleet of about 200 private cars in addition to the London Transport Board buses.

An astonishing feat! On the Wednesday evening another message came from the Home Office asking Miss Farrer to hold her fire. Talks were going better than expected in Munich and the evacuation plan would not be needed. She managed to cancel everything but one party of sixty children, who had been sent to her old Cambridge college, Newnham, and who were returned the following day. Peace in our time, said Chamberlain. Perhaps, thought the WI, and carried on with preparations for war.

The NFWI followed this with a survey of the homes of 16 million people prior to the war and set out proposals for evacuating children which included keeping groups of two to five year olds together in groups of ten with specialised staff and foster mothers. The need for after-school activities to keep older children out of mischief had been posited, and they warned against the resentment indiscriminate billeting would cause. They also pointed out that the formula of one person to one room, impossible in many cottages, meant that it would be the middle classes who bore the brunt of the exercise. The first few months following the declaration of war on 3 September 1939 became known as the phoney war, and the week war was declared Operation Pied Piper was launched. This involved moving 3 million vulnerable people from areas that might be bombed to parts of the country that might be safer. Unsurprisingly, the government ignored the WI's advice, which resulted, as Maggie Andrews has said, in the most almighty mess.

E. M. Delafield writes a fictionalised account of the sheer

disruption caused not only to the families sending their children away but to the families receiving them. She writes of the billeting officer ringing at all hours of the day and far into the night with information about arrival times which proved to be wrong; of an aged aunt who flees the insecurity of London but is stranded on the station platform because the train is late and the telegraph service is disrupted. Mrs Milburn's account shows no such disruption. They had already done a survey of who could offer accommodation, and this needed to be updated, which they duly did. Alongside this her son Alan received his call-up papers, so she arranged to go to the solicitor's so he could make his will. On Sunday 3 September 'it was bright and sunny and a really hot day by 10 a.m., when all billeting wardens were to be in their appointed places in the school playground to receive the teachers and children arriving from Coventry by bus.' Meanwhile Alan's room had to be prepared to take two adult evacuees, teachers who were coming with the children.

At last the buses came and queue after queue of clean and tidy children filed into the playground accompanied by many teachers. We allotted children to foster-parents as we consulted our survey books, took their names and went with them into a schoolroom where they were given a card to be handed to their foster-parent who later signed it as having received them.

One voice piped up. 'Please, miss, Sydney wants to be with his sister. He's only seven and she looks after him and puts him to bed.' People in small cottages couldn't accommodate a boy and a girl, but the situation was solved when someone offered to take Sydney and his sister went next door to a woman who wanted 'a nice, clean little girl to be with mine – and I must take one home today or my little girl will be so disappointed.'

Elsfield's experience accords more with E. M. Delafield than with Mrs Milburn. As Oxfordshire was deemed to be a county safe from German bombing, arrangements were made to evacuate London children to Oxfordshire villages, Elsfield among them. Helena Deneke was appointed billeting officer and arranged for five children to be taken in. Mrs Chaulk, Mrs Brown and Mrs Webb had all agreed to take one or two children depending on spare bedrooms. They waited all afternoon opposite the manor, having been told that the children would arrive in the early afternoon. The bus did not come till 6 p.m., and was driven by a surly driver. A biggish boy of fourteen went to Mrs Webb, two little girls to Mrs Chaulk. Miss Deneke asked where the other three children were. The driver jerked his head in the direction of Church Farm. Miss Deneke hurried in that direction and was confronted by an outraged Mrs Brown guarding the gate. She had agreed to take two school-age children but had been left with 'a most unprepossessing little mother with one baby in her arms, another clinging to her skirts and in the advanced stages of expecting a third'. Mrs Brown refused to take them in, which Miss Deneke could understand, given the busy life led by a farmer's wife. Miss Parsons agreed to take them in on a temporary basis. There was no antenatal clinic in Elsfield and no transport to get the mother to one, so she was eventually found a billet in the neighbouring village of Horspath and moved there. The mother had cried all the time – her unemployed husband had looked after the children and she didn't know how to do it and she didn't understand why the lady had told her to leave London. She went home before long, but Miss Parsons had had a distressing time and her good spare room mattress was spoilt. The whole affair had shocked and outraged her. The boy billeted with Mrs Webb proved too much of a handful. He was too old for Elsfield school and was transferred to Horspath, where his school was billeted along with his teacher. Mrs Chaulk cleaned the heads of the little girls and got them some extra clothes. She became quite fond of them and thought she had established a relationship with the parents, but the parents turned up one day and took the children back to London without even saying thank you. The reason for this monumental muddle was that the Great Western Railway had confused which train was going where. The train which should have gone to Oxford went to Weston-super-Mare, while the train which should have gone to Weston went to Oxford.

According to Miss Deneke, the later evacuation was much better planned. In the second wave of evacuations the twenty-five cottages were already full, so Miss Deneke had to turn again to the farms, which were the only houses with any spare capacity. These, however, were reserved for soldiers and land workers. Miss Parsons said 'with trembling lip' that she would take a 'nice mother and baby'. Lady Tweedsmuir had arranged her own evacuees, among them a Mrs Robinson, a London housing expert, who took over some of Miss Deneke's responsibilities. Nine further children were brought to Elsfield privately and proper billeting allowances were negotiated by Mrs Robinson. The vicarage, too, had self-evacuated people who came and went. The children from London were intelligent, Miss Deneke concluded, but unruly. Most were from Holborn and they missed fish and chips, the streets and the shops, and found it difficult to adapt to life in the country, so they didn't stay long.

At the end of 1939 Frances Farrer had sent a questionnaire out to the counties to ask for their experiences of taking in evacuees. She asked how many children there were in the house, where they came from and whether they suffered from head lice, skin disease, bed-wetting or other insanitary habits. She also asked about any accompanying mothers and whether they lacked the knowledge to bring up their children.

She was not short of replies. Some 1,700 branches filled in the questionnaire and catalogued in detail the shortcomings of the visitors forced on them by the exigencies of war. Most of them replicated what Miss Deneke had reported. They listed a lack of knowledge of childcare among the mothers, children who had to be cut out of their clothes, which had been stitched on to them who knew when, children with head lice, fleas and scabies. In Dorset, of the 849 children who arrived in Dorchester, 229 had lice, nineteen had skin diseases and forty-nine regularly wet the bed. It seems likely that bed-wetting as a reaction to stress would not have been understood by many people at the time, and Maggie Andrews tries to explain some of the discrepancies between town life and country life by saying that the first wave of evacuations took place at the end of the summer holidays, when many children had not had their heads inspected for lice for six weeks, and that the poor condition of their clothes could perhaps be accounted for by the fact that it was the end of the summer holidays and the children's clothes would have had a great deal of wear during that time. Generally speaking, however, many mothers would have thought it incumbent to inspect their children's heads every week and take appropriate action, poverty or no poverty. The unruliness of the children's behaviour can be explained not just by poor training on the part of the mother but by the situation. The adults could well have been confused about who was responsible for controlling the

Left: 1. A tense Lady Denman as a young woman, in evening dress. (Courtesy of the Mary Evans Picture Library)

Right: 2. The official face of Lady Denman in the 1930s.

3. Lady Denman on the beach with her granddaughter, 1935.

Left: 4. Grace Hadow, left, with Mrs Deneke, right.

Above: 5. Grace Hadow and her brother Harry, W. H. Hadow.

6. Grace Hadow, centre, as Everyman.

Above: 7. Forest Hill, Oxfordshire, WI Committee, 1935, published in their village history book.

Left: 8. Helena Deneke in 1919. (By kind permission of the Principal and Fellows of Lady Margaret Hall, University of Oxford)

9. Helena and Margaret Deneke with their dog Jackie, date unknown. (By kind permission of the Principal and Fellows of Lady Margaret Hall, University of Oxford)

10. Forest Hill WI, 1935.

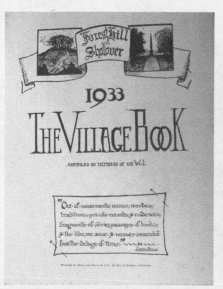

Left: 11. Forest Hill Local History Book, 1935.

Right: 12. One of the pages of a book presented to Lady Denman in 1937.

Above: 13. Fetching water from the pump in Elsfield, 1940s.

Right: 14. Susan Buchan, president of Elsfield WI, with her son Alistair and dogs Black Douglas and Spider. (Courtesy of Lord Tweedsmuir)

Below: 15. The then Duchess of York, later the queen and Queen Mother, watching a caning demonstration in 1938.

OXFORDSHIRE FEDERATION OF WOMEN'S INSTITUTES.

LIST OF LECTURES AND DEMONSTRATIONS AVAILABLE FOR
WOMEN'S INSTITUTES.

Further particulars will be found in the Panel of Speakers and Demonstrators.

LECTURES.

Acting
Architecture
Astronomy
Birds
Books
Broadcasting
Care of the blind
Care of mental defectives
Care of the teeth
Cinemas
Colour in the home
Community singing
Debates
Dickens
Drama
Education
Electricity
English History
Famous men and women
Fire

Flowers
Folk lore
Folk songs
Food and health
Gardens
George Eliot
Health and Hygiene
Herbs
History of pillow lace
Home nursing
Housing
How to keep fit
Humour
Jokes
League of Nations
Local Government
Local history
Mime
Music
Musical appreciation

Names
National savings
Nature talks
Novels
Old customs
Oxford
Oxfordshire
Penal reform
Pipe making and playing
Probation
Public questions
Puppetry
Rates and taxes
Roads
Social insurance
Travel talks
Travel talks with lantern
Trees
Water supply
Women police

TALKS OFFERED BY VOLUNTARY COUNTY ORGANISERS
ON INSTITUTE SUBJECTS.

How we govern ourselves
Money matters
Our responsibilities to one another
Programme planning. (Talk or Talk
and Round Table Conference)

Social half-hour
Spending each other's money
The good neighbour
The Institutes' account keeping

The members' share in the W.I.
programme
What the W.I. can do for the
village
Where are we going?

DEMONSTRATIONS.

Angora rabbits
Appliqué
*Basket work
Cake icing
*Canvas embroidery
Carpentry and house decorating
Carpet repairs
Chair seating
Chutney and pickles
Cookery
Cutting out
Dairy work
Decorative stitchery
*Dressmaking
*Embroidery
Feather mounting

Folding box making
Fruit bottling
*Fur craft
*Glove making
Goat keeping
Ham and Bacon curing
Home decorating
Household repairs
Household soap
Jam making
Knitting
Leather work
*Linen embroidery and cross-stitch
*Loose covers
Marmalade
Millinery

*Patch work
Papier maché
Pattern adapting
Pewter work
Poultry keeping
*Quilting
Raffia work
*Rug making
*Rush work
Soft slippers
Sweet making
*Upholstery
Use of cheaper joints
Use of an old mackintosh
Writing and illuminating

* Demonstrations marked * should be introductory to a class.

Before the year's programme is drawn up these lists should be given to the Members, who should be asked to mark the subjects they prefer, and return them before a fixed date.

16. List of lectures available for branches in Oxfordshire in the 1920s and 1930s.

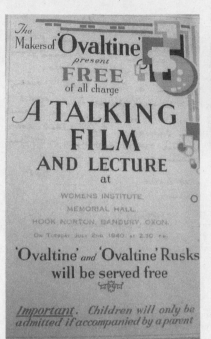

The Makers of 'Ovaltine'
present
FREE
of all charge

A TALKING FILM AND LECTURE
at

WOMENS INSTITUTE
MEMORIAL HALL
HOOK NORTON, BANBURY, OXON.

ON TUESDAY JULY 2ND 1940, AT 2.30 P.M.

'Ovaltine' *and* 'Ovaltine' Rusks
will be served free

Important. Children will only be
admitted if accompanied by a parent

Left: 17. An advertisement for a film about Ovaltine for Hook Norton WI in 1940.

Above: 18. A Berkshire bedroom made by WI members and shown in Reading and London at the NFWI Exhibition, 1932. (Courtesy of Berkshire Public Records Office)

Below: 19. A WI working party making fur coats from rabbit skins for the people of Russia, probably 1944.

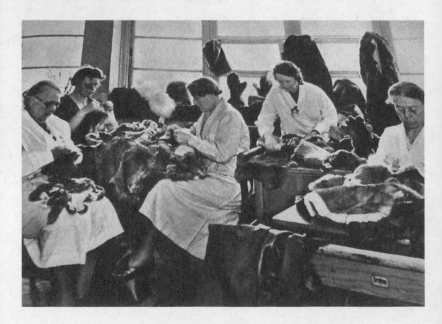

20. Shoes made from felt hats and deck-chair canvas, the work of a Dorset WI member, 1940s.

Left: 21. A WI market.

Right: 22. Malton WI market in the 1940s.

23. A demonstration of how to bottle fruit, 1940s.

Left: 24. Evacuee children leaving London, 1939.

Right: 25. Children evacuated to a Berkshire village with their teacher.

26. Brimpton WI preparing fruit for jam making, September 1941.

Left: 27. Making chutney at Springfield, Essex, in wartime.

Right: 28. Spindle-spinning wool gathered from the hedges in East Kent during the Second World War.

29. A herb-drying centre in Sussex during the Second World War. (Courtesy of the Women's Library, London School of Economics)

30. The queen in 1942 inspecting a canning unit at Reading. The unit was presented at a cost of £300 by American countrywomen through the British War Relief Society of America. (Courtesy of the Women's Library, LSE)

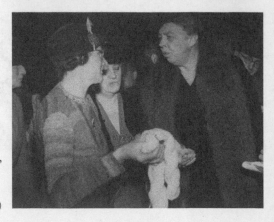

31. A rather unflattering photograph of Mrs Eleanor Roosevelt, on the right, wife of the American President Franklyn D. Roosevelt, talking to women of Barham WI in 1942. (Courtesy of the Women's Library, LSE)

CLOTHING FOR LIBERATED EUROPE

● COATS FOR CHILDREN UNDER TWO

COAT (Boy or Girl) Fifteen months to two years. Fig. A.

Fig. A.

MATERIALS:—5 oz. Wool. Two No. 9 Needles. Three Buttons.
MEASUREMENTS:—Length, 14 ins. Width, 23 ins. Length of sleeve (cuff turned up), 9 ins.
TENSION:—7 stitches to inch in width.
Commencing at lower edge of Right Front, cast on 50 stitches.
1st row.—K.1, (K.4, P.4) six times, K.1.
Repeat this row five times.
7th row.—K.1, (P.4, K.4) nine times, K.1.
Repeat 7th row five times.
13th row.—K.5, P.4, knit to end of row.
14th row.—K.1, purl to last 9 sts., K.4, P.4, K.1.
Repeat 13th and 14th rows twice.
Keeping a border of 2 blocks at front edge, work 26 rows without shaping.
In next row K.1, P.2, P.2 together, wool over needle (for button-hole), knit to end of row.

Still keeping border at front edge, continue without shaping, making a button-hole as before in every following 36th row until there are three button-holes in all.
Work 3 rows without shaping.
Cast off 16 sts. at beginning of next row.
Work one row without shaping.
Decrease once at neck edge in every row until 26 sts. remain.
Work 6 rows without shaping. Leave until Left Front has been worked.
Work Left Front to correspond with Right Front, including button-holes and ending with a purl row.

1
P.T.O.

32. A pattern for knitting a coat for a small child, to send to countries such as Greece and Holland in 1945.

Above: 33. The end of a course on caravanning held at Denman College in 1948. (By kind permission of *The Oxford Times*)

Right: 34. Elsfield WI banner.

Above left: 35. Marston WI banner.

Above right: 36. Clanfield WI banner.

Below left: 37. Garsington WI banner.

Below right: 38. Wootton WI banner.

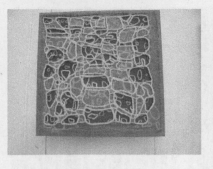

Above: 39. Osteoporosis panel worked by Jane Madden, Maureen White and members of Wolvercote WI.

Right: 40. Asthma panel worked by Judy Goodall and members of Chilton WI.

41. Diamond Light Source Centre with WI wall hangings either side of the stairs.

Above: 42. Members of Ottery St Mary WI at the Ottery Food Fair 2013. (By kind permission of Simon Horn)

Below left: 43. Judy Goodall on the left, with two other members of Chilton WI.

Below right: 44. Nail art at Tea Birds WI, Oxfordshire Federation, 2013.

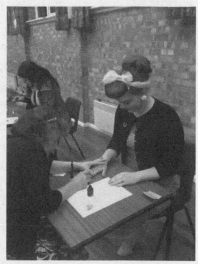

children, mothers thinking it was the responsibility of the hostess and the hostess thinking it was the responsibility of the mother. In cases such as this, children tend to sense the ambiguity and behave correspondingly badly.

Cicely McCall, who read and collated the experiences catalogued in the survey, wrote that what the country housewife found most upsetting about the whole experience was 'the parents' indifference to their children's dirt and disease'. She also underlines the difficulty for poor families to be housed by the lady of the manor, or for a child to be sent to an elderly pensioner or a childless couple who had never had any experience of looking after children. 'Under such circumstances evacuation could not be expected to be a success. It was unfair to both parties.' Maggie Andrews also points out that there were differences in the morality of survival in urban and rural settings. One boy came back to his billet one day with a live hen under his arm and told his landlady he could get plenty more for her, a tale told in the book which the WI produced from the questionnaire, *Town Children through Country Eyes*.

Experiences of evacuation and its effects on both hosts and evacuees demonstrated to many people that the state was failing a large number of its citizens and that if the war was worth fighting, the country needed to do more to care for its inhabitants in the post-war period. It may well have helped to fuel the demand for the setting up of the welfare state. *Town Children through Country Eyes* was read by a restricted number of people, but the information contained in it was used by Margaret Bondfield, a woman who had served as an MP in Ramsay Macdonald's Labour Cabinet in 1929. She wrote a preface to *Our Towns: A Close-up*, which was written in association with the National Council of Social Service and the Hygiene Committee of the Women's Group on Public Welfare, and was published in 1943. This reached a much wider audience than the WI publication.

The work of the WI during the war years was important for helping to build a consensus about the welfare reforms outlined in the Beveridge Report. There was a system which controlled everything. The milk supply was zoned so you could buy milk from only one named supplier, everyone had to register with a grocer and get their groceries only from that source, and the use of coupons ensured that everyone had their fair share of food and clothing. So central control, though often galling, did actually keep people fed, even if it was at the expense of individual freedom and spontaneity. This made the idea of central control of such matters as water supplies, electricity and rubbish collection much more acceptable in the post-war years. In 1943 Lady Denman spoke at the WI national conference, the only one in wartime, and reminded the federation of its role as a pressure group in politics. They should, she said, be looking towards the future and the end of the war, and gathering information from members about their ideas for education and what their requirements might be in a post-war world. One member had written to *Home and Country* in 1940 to express her astonishment that her village, which had been campaigning for running water and electricity for years, had had an army camp stationed near the village, the camp had had water and drainage immediately. Why couldn't this happen for ordinary people in peacetime, she wanted to know.

The Beveridge Report was seen by many members as a recognition of the importance of the housewife's role as a skilled worker. It introduced the idea of family allowances, widow's benefit, maternity grants and health care. In 1943 a resolution for the AGM said, 'This meeting records its appreciation of Sir

William Beveridge's great work for social security and particularly of his recognition that health insurance for housewives and family allowances are essential if family life is to be free of want.'

That same year Ernest Bevin and Winston Churchill acknowledged the contribution the WI had made to the country's war work. Miss Dorothy Elliott proposed a vote of thanks to Mr Churchill and said, 'We women hate war and we shall find our fullest opportunity for service in the peace for if you cannot win the war without women, neither can you win the peace.'

And what of Miss Wickham, that intrepid Hampshire VCO, during these tumultuous times? She was keeping calm and carrying on. 1940 found her in a house in Stockbridge where there was a meeting of ten members. The siren went in the middle of her talk on 'Better Health' and a dogfight developed overhead, so the hostess firmly closed the inside shutters and put on the lights, which after a bit went out and they were left in the dark. 'There was a very big bang followed soon after by the "All Clear". A German plane had been shot down in a field a few miles away. We abandoned "Better Health" and had a discussion on jam!', she wrote. The afternoon of D-Day, when the Allies launched their attack on Nazi-occupied France, found Miss Wickham travelling by train across Hampshire to give a talk to Newtown WI, near Newbury. For several weeks preceding this, she had carried a small card to give her permission to travel within an eighteen-mile stretch from the coast and on this occasion she remembers seeing coach after coach of Red Cross trains in every available siding. 'Overhead planes, towing huge gliders, circled round and round from their airfields nearby lining up for their journey to France.' The bus took her out to a garden meeting where members were sitting on the grass waiting to hear her talk on 'Stories and Legends'. 'I do not remember what stories and legends I told them and I do not suppose they remember either, as it was a bit of a battle anyway between my voice and the heavy droning noise of the planes in the sky above me!'

In 1945 Mrs Milburn's son came home, and her local WI, Berkswell, rang her up to say how pleased they were. Parties were arranged up and down the land to celebrate first Victory in Europe (VE) Day and later Victory over Japan (VJ) Day. The NFWI was now able to resume its annual meeting. In her speech on that occasion Lady Denman said how satisfied she was at the part the WI had played during the difficult years of the war. 'There has hardly been a government department which has not asked through our organisation for the help and co-operation of countrywomen,' she said. She congratulated the meeting that so many more WI members were now serving on local government bodies and that the surveys they had undertaken were strongly influencing official plans for rural improvement. The queen herself was present in her role as president of the Sandringham branch, and paid tribute to Lady Denman, congratulating her on all the WI had achieved under her leadership. 'I hope she realises the deep gratitude and affection which members feel for her,' she concluded. Trudie, now in her sixties, had just told the executive that she would not be standing for re-election as chairman and that they would have to look for another leader. She was happy to pass the baton on to Lady Albemarle. Lady Denman said in her farewell speech, 'I should like you to know that I think I have had an absolutely perfect job being your Chairman, because I think that countrywomen are the salt of the earth. I do not think they get a fair deal and I have always thought that if we got together we could do something about it. It has given me the greatest happiness.'

7

WINNING THE PEACE: THE POST-WAR
YEARS, 1945–1960

The years immediately following the war saw a huge increase in membership of the WI, following the return to civilian life of all the women who had been conscripted. By the end of 1946 there were 6,326 institutes with a membership of 303,000. This necessitated a recruitment drive for VCOs to support the new and expanded branches.

Surrey appointed four new VCOs, including a lady called Mrs Bloxham. Unfortunately the first thing Mrs Bloxham did as a VCO was to fall and break a leg, perhaps on the ice in that very bad winter. The weather made life difficult in other ways. Floods in Hertfordshire resulted in such disruption to the agenda conferences that only fifty-two people arrived at the St Albans meeting and fifty-four at Hatfield, where the speakers didn't arrive till the end of the meeting, having been rescued from the floods by a combination of a tractor and POWs who dug them out when they got stuck. Snow in Staffordshire prevented the speaker arriving at Adbaston, but showing a high degree of lateral thinking, two members went out and killed and plucked a chicken, which another member demonstrated how to dress!

Looking back from the perspective of the 1990s, Jane Lewis, in her book *Women in Britain since 1945*, has itemised three social trends which were significant for women at this time: an increase in the percentage of married women in paid employment, a dramatic increase in divorce and issues around women's control of their own fertility. What she doesn't mention is the fluctuations in population levels, the improvement in living standards and the Americanisation of British culture, all of which had an effect on women in general and the WI in particular.

These social trends are all linked, so it is difficult to disentangle one from another, but let us start with population levels. Before the war the government had been concerned that with working-class access to contraception the population was falling. A study by Enid Charles, published under the dramatic title of *The Twilight of Parenthood* in 1934, had predicted that by the year 2000 the population of England and Wales would shrink to the size of London then. The social dislocation brought about by the war and before that the depression in the 1930s was thought to have destroyed family life and the decline in the birth rate and an increase in juvenile delinquency was thought to prove it.

One of the tasks for the post-war world was not just to rebuild the housing stock after the bombing, but to encourage the reconstruction of family life. By this reckoning women should be back in the home being good housewives, producing lots of children and giving them a good upbringing. Up to the Second World War married women made up only 10 per cent of the workforce, but a 1943 survey showed that three-quarters of professional women wanted to keep their jobs, while women doing monotonous jobs disliked them and would like to stop work outside the home.

Research published by psychiatrists D. Winnicott and John Bowlby, who had made detailed studies of the effect of separation on mothers and babies, showed how damaging separation could be to both mother and baby if they were separated for any length of time. Winnicott said in a radio broadcast, 'Talk about women not wanting to be housewives seems to me just nonsense because nowhere else but in her own home is a woman in command.' (Oh dear!) The message was clear: children needed full-time mothering, otherwise they would grow up delinquent, and there was no room for women to take responsibility outside the home. So there were tremendous pressures for women to return to the domestic scene. Good mothering moved up the political agenda and the government decided matters for many women by closing many of the day nurseries that had provided for the children of working mothers during the war, 50 per cent of which had been closed by 1955.

As Jane Lewis again points out, 'The prime measure of family efficiency has remained the degree to which the family demonstrates its capacity to care for its members and to socialise its children.' The WI accepted that women's most vital role was that of motherhood, and women were advised to work up to the birth of their first child and not again until after the children had left school. There was a shortage of teachers, so the regulations about their employment were relaxed. Teachers could now teach after they had married but were expected to resign if they became pregnant. There was also a great deal of secretarial work to be had, which was deemed suitable for women, so there were jobs available for anyone who wanted to work. The topic was discussed at branch level by some

WIs – 'Should women have a career after marriage?' – and the discussion went on well into the 1950s.

There is a letter in the WI archive from the Winchester branch to the then administrative head of the National Federation, Dame Frances Farrar. They were seeking guidance on what to do about a letter they had received from the Winchester Diocesan Council for Moral Welfare, which had asked their support for a motion that 'Conference views with deep concern the statements given by Police and Moral Welfare experts that young children whose parents are at work are liable to physical and moral dangers when left unattended from the time they leave school to the time when parents return from their work.' The letter states that 'several people round the table knew personally of cases where village children had been molested', an early expression of concern about the sexual abuse of children.

An economic survey in 1947 suggested that employers should 'adjust the conditions of work to suit, as far as possible, the convenience of women with household responsibilities'. One response to this was to provide 'twilight' shifts so women could work in the evenings after a day spent working in the home. By the 1950s women had started taking time out of work to have their children then returning to part-time work when their children were older. In the course of the 1950s the percentage of married women in the workforce went from 26 per cent in 1951 to 35 per cent in 1960. The trend continued upwards, with 49 per cent in 1971 and 64 per cent in 1985. In 1957 the National Council of Women of Great Britain, to which the WI is affiliated, produced a study of married women and working practices. They found, unsurprisingly, that most women worked for the money, because living costs were increasing. Rents were higher, but people also wanted to spend money on good clothes, toys and television sets. There was no indication that women were going out to work for company, but they did work to have economic independence, which they had often been accustomed to before marriage. The study came down heavily on the side of the working mothers. 'Certainly no case was made that the mere fact of a woman going out to work is detrimental to her home and family,' they state firmly. They point out that school dinners are a great help to the working mother, as is the lightening of the burden of domestic work, which, with new machines such as washing machines and vacuum cleaners, is considerably lighter than before the war. They do, however, suggest that there should be more after-school provision. One unforeseen result of women's lesser economic dependence on their husbands was a change in the family dynamics, making women less financially dependent on husbands. This would have interesting consequences in the following decade.

There was a shortage of workers, in part due to the arrival of the welfare state, with administration deemed suitable work for women. The gap in the numbers of people prepared to work in low-paid jobs was in some cases filled by displaced persons, or DPs as they were known. A letter in *Home and Country* asked for people to befriend the many Latvian and Lithuanian displaced persons who were working in sanatoria as domestics, because these women were lonely and would welcome the friendship of the native population, and in 1948 the SS *Windrush* brought an influx of people from the Caribbean, many of whom found work in the newly established NHS.

In the immediate aftermath of the war life was still difficult. The maintenance of rationing was a source of irritation to many housewives and the introduction of bread rationing in 1946, which lasted till 1948, was an additional irritant. Clothing coupons were abolished in 1949, a relief to young mothers who had had to use twelve of their precious clothing coupons for nappies. Nylon stockings were difficult to come by, too. In Southampton it was said you only had nylons if your husband was a sea captain or if you were a prostitute.

Home and Country carried a valiant column by Philip Harben. Although his name will be unknown to younger people, he was the first of the celebrity chefs on television. He had been invalided out of the RAF with an eye injury, and drafted into the catering corps. In 1942 he began compering a BBC cookery programme and by 1946 moved to television, where he presented *Cookery*. He wrote many cookery books between then and his death in 1970, so it was something of a coup on the part of *Home and Country* to get him to write for them. He made heavy use of dried egg and sardines in his recipes. One idea, which shows how people had to adapt to shortages of such basics as oil and fats, was to drain the oil from a tin of sardines, mix it with two teaspoons of HP sauce and fry the sardines in that, and serve them on toast as devilled sardines. He also described how to cook a pike, which he assured his readers was delicious. On the page opposite his column is an advertisement for Winox, 'for weak digestions!' – a judicious placing! In 1947 the government allowed farmers who had been forced to grow cereal crops to revert to dairy farming, which meant an increase in the availability of butter, cheese and meat. By 1949 Philip Harben was providing recipes for meringues and using lemons for flavouring in cakes, real vanilla pods and butter!

There was a lively correspondence about washing up, which points out the difficulties shortages were posing. There had been an article on the subject from Major Philipson-Stowe recommending using three bowls, two of them enamelled and twelve to fourteen inches in diameter. One reader, Erskine Wyse, who through wedlock, as he put it, found himself regimented into the Loyal Corps of Scullions, said he couldn't find space for three washing-up bowls, and as for raising a 'good lather in the washing up bowl', his soap ration wouldn't run to it. A further letter suggested that to overcome the problem of lack of soap, Erskine Wyse should use a soap saver – a basket to take odd scraps of soap which were too small to use ordinarily.

In 1945 the British public had voted against the Conservative Party led by Winston Churchill and for the Labour Party led by Clement Attlee, a quiet, pipe-smoking ex-lawyer. During the five years of that Labour government, momentous changes took place. Services such as water, electricity, gas and the railways were nationalised, and with the abolition of fees grammar schools were opened up to working-class children.

Perhaps the most momentous change was the establishment of the National Health Service in 1948. The very face of the country was changing. From now on there would be no need for the WI to raise funds for the local hospital – it would be paid for out of National Health contributions. In 1947 Mr Tom Williams from the Ministry of Agriculture and Fisheries foresaw the time when, with the advent of electricity in the villages, the rural housewife

will be able to use all the most up-to-date electric appliances – cookers, irons, washers, vacuum cleaners, heaters etc. all of which improve year upon year. By eliminating the dirt and work caused by ancient cooking ranges and the oil lamp, these will make her life brighter, more pleasant and more free. It will be possible for her to have a decently lit house during the winter and to listen to a mains-operated radio while she is working and resting.

This idyll seemed to some readers to be a long time coming.

Outside earth closets, which should have been a thing of the past in 1949, were the subject of a survey undertaken by the National Federation. They reported that in many places matters were no better than they had ever been. In Acton Trussell in Staffordshire, 'Two hundred people are without proper water supplies and sanitation. Water has to be carried a quarter of a mile and then boiled.' In Alleborough in Lincolnshire there were twelve council houses where the sewerage outflow 'runs down the village street'. 'The smell', they add, 'is appalling.' Also included in the survey is a review of the sanitary arrangements in schools, which makes interesting reading. In Eversden in Cambridgeshire the school had bucket-type sanitation 'with no doors', the recorder adds. 'The teacher uses the same toilet facilities so she has to lock the children in the school while she uses the conveniences, which are in full view of the school.' Not easy to maintain your dignity and keep the respect of your pupils in a situation such as this! The survey for the schools in Cheshire, which covered ninety-four villages, showed that fifty-five had mains water, ten had pump, well or spring water. Twelve had main drainage, ten had a tank or cesspit while forty-two had earth or pail closets. One school had a cess pit which had been emptied once in seventeen years, another had rainwater for washing and drinking water from a spring on a muddy lane 150 yards away.

In spite of the many difficulties, electricity, mains water and sewerage did arrive in rural Britain. Villages that had struggled through the first half of the century on candles, oil lamps and paraffin, a fact pointed out in Garsington's account of the banner they made in the 1930s 'by candle- and lamp-light', were now lit by electricity. WI members could knit to their hearts' content in the light of the bulb dangling from the ceiling and food could be cooked in an electric oven rather than on the open fire or in the fireside oven.

With the establishment of the welfare state women had gained much of what the WI had campaigned for in the years before the war. There was universal health care, and the higher echelons of education were open to the more intellectual among them, though there were many fewer places available at Oxford and Cambridge for women than for men. Electricity, water and sewerage had been brought to the villages and there was a bus service which, though often seen as less than adequate, would get them from the village to the nearest town or city. Of course there were drawbacks to this idyll. For one thing, there was a very long gap – or so it seemed to everyone – between an act being passed and any sign of action on the village street.

There were shortcomings in the legislation, too. Sir William Beveridge, along with most people in the 1930s, had assumed that a married woman, whether she had children or not, would not go out to paid work, so she could be classified as a dependant, her benefits being made payable through her husband's insurance. Beveridge, and much of society, considered the husband as breadwinner and the wife as (unpaid) carer of the young and the old in the family. There was no need, therefore, for women to be paid the same amount as men for the same amount of work, since men had to support a family and in theory women had only themselves to support. The Labour government did not bring in equal pay for equal work at this point.

Even with the establishment of the welfare state, there was a sense of disappointment that the Labour government had not provided everything people had expected of it. Life was getting better, with petrol rationing ending in 1950, but even so, people were disappointed at the rate of change. The Labour Party called an election in 1950 when their majority was much reduced and in the following year, 1951, held another election – the Conservative Party under the leadership of Winston Churchill won this election. Sweet rationing was lifted in 1953, as was sugar rationing, and it began to feel like the country was returning to normal.

At this time *Home and Country* expected their readers to be interested in politics and regularly reported on parliamentary matters that affected their members. In March 1947, for example, they recorded that a question had been asked in Parliament about increasing the number of slaughterhouses, to improve the supply of meat and to lessen the suffering of the animals. Dr Edith Summerskill, of the Ministry of Food, reported that where suitable premises were available they would be opened, but many of pre-war slaughterhouses had been in the back yards of butchers' shops, with access to them only through the shop. These, she replied sternly, would not be re-opened. A further example is a short paragraph stating that people could now apply for a shortened birth certificate, which would not give their parentage. This was aimed at disguising the stigma of illegitimacy, which was such a social handicap people could lose their jobs if born out of wedlock.

For the women of the WI, while they of course participated in the general improvement in living in the post-war era, there were losses. They lost much of the immediate access and influence their leaders had had on the government of the time. Labour Cabinet ministers had no intention of listening to what WI ladies – Denman, Albemarle or Brunner – had to say, though Lady Brunner was called to the Board of Trade to inform the minister about the hardships WI members were suffering – the lack of bed linen, country shoes and Wellington boots. They also told of the difficulty of not being able to sell rationed goods at jumble sales and the restrictions on the distribution of gift clothing from overseas. Sir Stafford Cripps, the President of the Board of Trade, took time out from his ministerial duties to address the conference at the AGM in 1947. He pointed out that while it was difficult with so many goods being in short supply, the country was still borrowing from America and Canada and the country was short of raw materials and labour. He knew that children's shoes and prams were particularly difficult. But it was essential for the government to keep a tight hold on everything so what was available did not go to those with the most money.

The WI was ideally situated to collect information about living conditions in the countryside, and while it was not always easy to affect government policy, they could and did act at the local level. In 1956 Cicely McCall, education officer for the NFWI, sent out a questionnaire about the conditions in the villages, which she then analysed and published. She asked about housing, water supplies, sewerage and electricity, the prevalence of the home help service, out-patient clinics, children in hospital, the bus service, the footpaths and the provision of litter bins. The question about housing elicited examples of wash houses built without water, ventilation or daylight, larders next to hot tanks, and houses with baths upstairs when the only source of water was downstairs. Then she asked for the branches to prioritise what was most urgently needed. Compared with two previous surveys in 1944 and 1950, she notes that water moved right down the list to number six, but road safety was now a priority. After questions about services such as sewerage and electricity, the local bus service and other matters of pressing concern, there is a final question: What has your institute done to try and get these improvements? Not only does she describe the results but she demonstrates to anyone reading her booklet, *Our Villages*, the methods employed: organising petitions, fundraising for a particular project, political pressure on local councillors and the MP, inviting people to their meetings – the district sanitary inspector, the chief constable, the chairman of the district council and the matron of the local hospital.

The WI also looked beyond their immediate members to women in the wider community. Following the AGM resolution of 1946, Norfolk County Federation undertook a survey to investigate the provision for the elderly in their communities. They recommended that for the elderly but not infirm there should be small bungalows or flats with resident wardens who would keep an eye on the residents. They would also need visitors to bring news of the outside world so they did not feel isolated and lonely. For those who needed residential care, old people's homes should allow people to keep their belongings around them and to have their own clothes. This may today seem to be stating the obvious, but 1947 was not so far removed from the workhouses for the indigent, where men and women were accommodated in separate blocks and where they were assigned a uniform. And it has to be said that in the daily life of care homes, while the intention may be for people to have their own clothing, they may well not keep them. Clothes go in the washer, then the dryer, and unless the person sorting the washing is very clued up about the inmates and knows who owns what, it is very difficult to ensure that clothes are returned to their rightful owners.

The WI considered one of its areas of concern to be that of health. The main aim of a woman's work was to keep the home clean so as to ensure the health of her family, to make sure children were properly fed and clothed, meals were on the table for the man of the house when he returned from work and the old people in the family were properly cared for. Since the 1930s the WI had been concerned about the provision of analgesics – gas and air – which were available to pregnant women who went into labour in the towns but not to women in rural communities. This was a battle that was still ongoing in the 1950s. The WI took matters into their own hands in Llansawel in 1950 when they raised money for an analgesia outfit for the district nurse and thereby no doubt received the gratitude of the young women of the village.

The WI was also interested in the health of the community, including sexual health. There had been considerable anxiety in the 1930s about what was perceived as an increase in venereal diseases, though in fact these had fallen to a historically low level by 1939, and this anxiety, which should have been assuaged by the invention of sulphonamides in 1937, had actually been accentuated by the arrival of American GIs during the war years. Concern about VD survived the war and one of the motions at the AGM in 1949 urged that treatment for venereal disease be included in NHS provision. Another motion urged the Home Secretary to provide homes where mothers convicted of offences involving ill treatment or neglect of their children could stay with their babies for training in housecraft.

The improvements in living conditions and the prosperity of the 1950s led to a dramatic increase in life expectancy. In 1951 men could expect to live to be sixty-six and women seventy, and by the end of the decade a man's lifespan would be sixty-eight and a woman's seventy-three. The mid-fifties also saw the development of vaccines against polio and tuberculosis, which, coupled with the development of antibiotics such as penicillin and its derivatives, lifted people's anxieties about their children's health.

In the 1950s many women, and certainly those in the WI, continued to believe that domesticity was their proper role in life. However, this was not a passive role but an active and assertive one. For many women consumerism was the way forward. Women saw themselves as 'discerning and critical buyers expressing their expertise', as Maggie Andrews put it. The skills which good housewives had always had – picking out the best vegetables to buy and the best value cuts of meat – were extended to the white goods that became available. WI members became experts in consumerism.

Life for the stay-at-home housewife was busy. Shopping had to be done every day, because very few people had fridges. There were no supermarkets, so shopping took longer, though increasingly there was an influx of machines to do much of the hard work previously done by hand, washing machines and vacuum cleaners being the main items releasing women from the drudgery of housework. As early as 1947 *Home and Country* carried an advertisement for the Acme wringer. A sixteen-inch model would set you back eighty-four shillings plus purchase tax, but it promised to make life much easier. No more wringing clothes by hand. Here was a new and up-to-date handy little machine which fastened to the top of your wash tub. All you had to do was turn the handle and push the clothes through the wringer. In fact it was no better than the cumbersome old mangles which people had been using, but was considerably more streamlined and took up much less room.

The 1950s began with the Festival of Britain, which was a surprisingly low-key event in WI circles. Women were urged to celebrate the festival in their own areas by singing the cantata for female voices by Vaughan Williams, *Folk Songs of Four Seasons*, and they ran a competition for a poem, one of which appears in *Home and Country*. Written by Marjorie K. Taylor, of Meary and Sheepstor WI, Devon, it begins, 'From lonely farms we greet you' and concludes with a couplet which probably expresses what the WI feels about Britain:

> Remember Britain's countryside
> Which cradles Britain's soul.

Their enthusiasm and energy were directed at the Ideal Home Exhibition, which was held at Olympia in March of 1951. Lady Brunner and other members of the executive had formed a working party with an architect to design and present the WI Ideal Home, which 140,000 people visited, after queuing for an hour and a half. It was a detached house with casement windows. Upstairs there were three bedrooms and a bathroom, while downstairs there was a hall big enough to take a pram with ease, a parlour, complete with toys and books, and a dining-kitchen. The kitchen contained all the latest gadgets: a fridge, an electric cooker, a range and a worktop with cupboards beneath. The roof was well insulated, the bedrooms heated by radiators run from a fireback boiler in the parlour, and the whole building was designed to be economical to run. What people liked best were the bedrooms and the covered access to the outhouse and laundry, with its electric clothes dryer. They found the parlour and bathroom too small. No garage, of course, because only really well-off people had cars.

The WI was also involved in the design and quality of household goods via their representative at a conference on consumer protection. The British Kitemark system was developed by the

British Standards Institute and the WI was involved with looking at the safety of electric cookers and the design of school uniforms. One of the strengths of the WI was its attention to detail. In the mid-1950s it was concerned with discussions about the quality and design of household goods. It concerned itself with the alignment of patterns on printed cloth, fast dyes for the linings of children's shoes, the length of stockings, fast dyes for industrial overalls and even the knots in knitting wool and the quality of sewing cottons. They spoke with authority and their views were respected and acted upon. They pressed for the sizing of garments to be standardised, as they were in America.

In parallel with their interest in consumer goods was an interest in what happened to the packaging of goods. A resolution at the 1954 AGM concerned the mess that was affecting the countryside from the disposal of packaging. This was not a new idea. In the 1930s Lady Tweedsmuir, president of Elsfield WI, had expressed her distress at the amount of wrappers and other rubbish that found its way into the hedges and ditches around her village. 'If only,' she said, 'manufacturers could make wrapping which would rot away quickly!' The 'Keep Britain Tidy' pressure group was formed in 1955 and is still active today. Here was something the branches could really get their teeth into. Hampshire Federation formed a 'coach spotters' team to keep an eye on coach parties who chucked their rubbish out of the coach windows, while Shropshire reproached British Rail Hotel executives for allowing its dining-car staff to jettison their rubbish out of the train windows.

Society was changing in other ways, too. In the 1920s and 1930s the WI had prided itself on its Englishness, its defence of the values represented by the English village. This identification with the 'country' side of 'home and country' had naturally enough been accentuated during the war when the WI, the Home Guard and the WVS had been seen as, and were, the stalwarts who kept the home fires burning. During and following the war there was an influx of migrants from Europe: Italians, Poles, Greeks, Ukrainians. The Italians brought their coffee bars with them and teenagers, a new category of society, spent many an hour in the *Roma* or the *Moka* drinking weak coffee or orange squash but more importantly meeting members of the opposite sex. Because of the unprecedented full employment, boys and girls leaving school had immediate access to a variety of jobs, all paying well, without the tediousness of an apprenticeship with its seven years' training and low pay. For the first time youngsters had money in their pockets, which they wanted to spend. They weren't interested in the values of old England, they wanted fun, colour, the excitement of the new. And this new world came very largely from America.

Before the war there had been the beginnings of an Americanisation of certain aspects of British life, most notably with the influx of American films, which brought American terminology, American history with its dramatic tales of the years of prohibition or the settling of the West, and knowledge of American glamour to Europe. During the war there had been American GIs with their chewing gum to endear them to children and their silk stockings and jazz to endear them to the women of the country. This was a tide that would become a torrent in the decades following the war. Music was one of the areas affected. The fifties began with crooners such as Bing Crosby and Frank Sinatra, who were very soon eclipsed by the star of rock 'n' roll, Elvis Presley, whose film, *Love Me Tender*, arrived on these shores in 1956 following his hit single *Heartbreak Hotel*.

It was difficult for the WI to counteract these trends. But one event where the WI felt completely at home was when one of their own, the Princess Elizabeth, was crowned queen in 1953. Lady Brunner, in her AGM speech in coronation year, put the emphasis on the future, not the past.

> Today we begin a new reign which has to be given its own quality
> ... [Families] look to a new era with its own excellence and virtue,
> its own poets and writers and musicians and painters, and they
> will see that contemporary history is a rich and vivid heritage and
> an inspiration to posterity, not a second hand rehash of individual
> splendours of the reigns of Queen Elizabeth I and Queen Victoria.

The cover of the souvenir edition of *Home and Country*, priced at four pence, was for the first time in colour, with a magnificent picture of heralds on horseback. There were photographs of the royal family, of Queen Elizabeth wearing her WI membership badge and of the can of plums packed, sealed and initialled by the queen mother, then the queen, which was sent to Mrs Roosevelt, wife of the President of the USA.

Philip Harben, in a flight of fancy unlikely to have been copied by many people, devised a coronation cake decorated with diamond-shaped pieces of jelly cut from the sides of a table jelly. He warned that they were tricky to cut. On no account must you saw the jelly or you would get grooves in it and the slices must be a minimum of an eighth of an inch thick otherwise they were impossible to handle. The coronation cake made by Colbury WI in Hampshire looked more appealing finished off with a crown on top. The purple velvet of the crown was made by colouring the mixture with blackcurrant juice, the ruby was a cherry, emeralds were of angelica and – *pièce de résistance* – the ermine was white icing studded with liquorice. Top marks for ingenuity, though perhaps not for taste!

The 1950s were a period which led the Conservative prime minister, Harold MacMillan, to tell people in 1957, 'You've never had it so good.' And he was right. The fifties, as Neil Kinnock has pointed out, were a time when there was 'security, opportunity and care with a breadth and depth previously unknown'. For the WI it was a time of readjustment to the realities of life in a welfare state when many of their goals had been achieved.

While the world as represented by the WI may have appeared a peaceful place in the fifties, it was not so on the world stage. The 1950s had seen the development of the Cold War, a struggle for power waged not directly but through confrontations which flared up from time to time between the Soviet Union and the USA. The Berlin blockade in 1948, the Korean War which began the 1950s, the Suez Crisis in 1956 and the formation of the Campaign for Nuclear Disarmament in 1958 were all ignored by the WI. While such matters would not have been expected to be discussed in the women's magazines of the period, and while the emphasis of the work of the WI has always been with the welfare of women on the domestic front, it comes as something of a disappointment that *Home and Country* never tackles in any way these momentous issues. One is given the feeling of a cosy, home-centred organisation which approaches such matters in such an oblique way that the links between the reality of the Cold War and the content of *Home and Country* are barely visible. There is a competition, for instance, to write an essay on 'How the organisation to which I belong is contributing to World Peace', won by Yvonne Brown of Harpsden in Oxfordshire, who thinks that 'like charity, international work begins at home'. She speaks of peace through understanding and that the WI 'by their efforts to spread mutual sympathy and trust between country women of different nationalities, are surely contributing valuable work in the cause of humanity'. There are also attempts to come to terms with atomic power, with a course at Denman on 'The Atom' – the peaceful use of atomic power, and an account of a visit to 'The Atom 1957' exhibition.

A momentous decade for the country and for the WI itself. How would it fare in the following decades of the century?

8

MISER ELWES'S NOT-SO-STATELY
HOME: DENMAN COLLEGE

You would have thought that in 1943, while the British Army battled its way along the coast of North Africa towards Egypt, the WI, dealing on the Home Front with food production, knitting for the troops, collecting salvage and making jam, would have had enough to think about without considering what would happen after the war and where the WI was heading.

That year, however, saw a meeting of almost a hundred delegates from branches throughout the country at Radbrook College in Shrewsbury. They were there to discuss education and social security in post-war Britain. Two members of the National Federation staff headed the delegation: Elizabeth Christmas and Cicely McCall. Elizabeth Christmas, or Betty as she was known to her friends, was a general organiser, while Cicely McCall was organiser to the education subcommittee, in which capacity she had travelled around the country arranging day schools on education and the planning of the future welfare state. In their working parties delegates discussed what the speaker, Liberal MP Clement Davies, had to say about the Beveridge Report of

1942. Their conclusions on such matters as health insurance and maternity grants would be forwarded to the author of the Beveridge Report, Sir William Beveridge himself. Another speaker was Sir Richard Livingstone, an Oxford don and an expert on adult education. He suggested that there had been a serious omission in the Education Bill (which led to the Education Act of 1944 introducing free secondary education for all children), and that omission was adult education. Primed by Betty Christmas and Cicely McCall, he suggested that the WI could have its own further education college. The idea was taken up by the delegates and a motion was passed that the WI should explore this idea – it was passed with enthusiasm.

While there was a lot of support for the idea of a college, there were also a considerable number of people who had reservations. Many branches in the North felt that the college would be established in the south and they would have little access to it, and several members of the executive expressed doubts about how the place would be funded. Even Lady Denman had doubts. 'Do you really think the members want a college?' she asked. The pro-college group, among them Lady Brunner, a new member of the committee from Oxford, was the granddaughter of the famous actor Henry Irving. She had had a career on the stage before marrying the banker Sir Felix Brunner and becoming mother to four sons, and she was determined to follow up the idea.

The idea of residential courses was not new. VCOs had been trained on residential courses based in various establishments around the country – in the 1920s Phyllis Wickham had travelled from Sutton Scotney in Berkshire to Broxbourne in Essex to be trained – and these courses proved popular, so this was only an extension of that idea.

All thoughts of an AGM had to be set aside in 1944 because of the flying bombs raining down on London, but Lady Brunner and Helena Deneke drafted a resolution from the Oxfordshire Federation to urge the national executive to pursue the idea. This was one of over a hundred resolutions that went forward for the 1945 AGM, only fourteen of which could be selected. The resolution suggesting a WI college be founded was one of the fourteen. Lady Brunner's stage experience stood her in good stead as she faced the audience, which filled the Albert Hall to capacity. She sketched out her vision for the college: a place which would be welcoming and homely where women could learn new skills and hone old ones, where all manner of different courses would be on offer to women from all over Britain. It would be inspirational. It might attract a grant from the Ministry of Education, but branches must be prepared to support their own college themselves.

The Shropshire Federation opposed the motion on the grounds that many women would find it impossible to leave their families and they were not convinced that local authorities would give grants for such a project. East Kent was likewise unconvinced, saying that 'the average countrywoman has neither the time nor the money to spare for long journeys'. They felt members could get all they needed from the county. The member for South Stoke, Betty King, poor woman, is remembered more for the fact that she had forgotten to change her gardening shoes and so appeared on stage in front of hundreds in battered old clompers, than for the fact that she supported the motion. She had practised her speech in the corridor of the train on the way up and must have been delighted that in spite of the gardening shoes the meeting voted overwhelmingly for the establishment of a college of its very own.

The 1946 AGM was notable for two things: Elizabeth Brunner

launched an appeal to raise £60,000 for the purchase, equipping and endowment of the college, and after fifty years as president Lady Denman announced her retirement from her post. Lady Albemarle, Lady Denman's heir apparent, proposed that a very good way to mark Lady Denman's association with the WI would be for the college to be named after her. 'We want this to be a memorial, of the sort that would appeal to her,' said Diana Albemarle. This met with the vociferous agreement of the whole meeting.

It was not easy to find a suitable house. Many country houses had been requisitioned during the war and had not yet been decommissioned. There was also a considerable amount of money which needed to be raised. The college subcommittee had already approached the Carnegie Trust, who promised £20,000 if the WI could raise the same amount itself. Purley Park near Reading came on the market and Lady Denman was so sure it was the right kind of building at a reasonable price that she put down the deposit herself. She was outvoted on the college subcommittee, however, and not long afterwards a member from Berkshire whose husband was an estate agent pointed out that Marcham Park was about to come on the market.

Marcham Park was known as the home of the eighteenth-century eccentric Miser Elwes. He was renowned for his ability to ignore physical discomfort – he refused to spend money on his roof, which leaked, and when he died in 1789 he was found lying in bed, with his shoes on his feet, his stick in his hand and a torn old hat on his head.

When the WI inspected the building it was in rather better shape than it had been in the eighteenth century, in spite of having been occupied by the RAF. The RAF were about to move out and when they saw it Lady Brunner and her co-members thought it would be very suitable. It still had blacked-out windows on the ground floor and there were Nissen huts and a concrete blockhouse in the grounds, but generally the property had not suffered too much. Elizabeth Brunner and Diana Albemarle were shown round by William Blackwell, a local man who had looked after the property before the war and had been retained during the war by the RAF. They were impressed by the elegant proportions of the downstairs rooms and the ten bedrooms on the first floor and six on the second. The stable block and the large kitchen garden could also, they felt, be put to good use. The Berners family, who owned it, were asking £16,000, which the national executive felt they could pay. This price included not only the house but a hundred acres of land, two cottages let to tenants and the kitchen garden and glass houses, which were let to a local market gardener. Although it was a huge amount of money, this was a time of great expansion for the WI, with new branches being formed at the rate of two or three a week. In addition, membership of existing branches was rising with the return of women from the forces and those giving up their war work. So the national executive was optimistic about raising the money needed for the establishment of what was now being thought of as Denman College. The RAF was ready to move out by June 1947, and in March 1948 the deal was concluded, half the purchase price being paid by the Carnegie UK Trust.

The first move was to second a secretary from head office, Margaret Bucknall, to deal with the paperwork. It was more difficult to get to grips with the physical alterations and repairs which needed to be done. A gardener, Miss Clarke, was found who was prepared to work for £4 a week. Along with two German POWs, she would bring the wilderness of a garden into some kind of shape. The committee had been hoping to raise money from selling off timber from the woodland, but a forestry expert called in to value the timber informed them that most of the valuable wood had already been sold. The stables had never been used for horses – instead it had acted as a storage unit for gas masks, but there was no hope of making the stable block into bedroom accommodation because all building work required a licence, there being a shortage of building materials in post-war Britain, and even if a licence were obtained the local builder would have no labour available. In spite of much lobbying by Elizabeth Brunner at the Ministry of Works this was not forthcoming, so the committee decided to make the best of a bad job and use the house alone for sleeping accommodation. At least they were given permission to repair the roof and the sewerage system!

Furnishing the building was done by individual county organisations. The Oxford Federation agreed to furnish the library in memory of Grace Hadow, while East Anglian branches furnished the entrance hall. Staffordshire, being the heart of the potteries, agreed to provide the crockery while Wiltshire sent several hundred clothing coupons for household linens, which were still rationed. There was still quite a lot of money in the bank. Some 4,000 branches had raised £41,000 in two years, and as there were now over 6,000 branches in existence, the £60,000 goal Elizabeth Brunner had set seemed to be well within reach.

By the end of April 1948 the house and gardens were felt to be sufficiently prepared for there to be an inspection by delegates of the AGM so that they could go back to their branches and tell them about the college. The 750 delegates were in London, however, and Denman College was two hours' coach ride away. But a WI husband was on hand to deal with the problem. Colonel

Yeo, whose wife Joan chaired the education subcommittee, had been in charge of troop movements on the Clyde during the war, so moving a large number of women across country was not much of a challenge. Twenty-four coaches in groups of three carrying thirty-two passengers apiece departed from London, each person having a colour-coded ticket. Each group was allowed two and a half hours to inspect the college and grounds, have a meal and get back on the bus ready to be whisked back to London.

The college now needed a warden, someone friendly and well organised who could make people feel at home. Betty Christmas was appointed. Unlike many of the people involved with Denman College up to this point, Betty was an ordinary working woman. The daughter of a village postmaster in West Sussex, she had first joined the WI so she could join in the amateur dramatics. She was soon appointed assistant secretary to the branch, and there came to the attention of the president, who was on the national executive. She soon moved to the national executive office in London. In 1945 she had toured Canadian WIs from coast to coast on behalf of the Ministry of Information, though her name had proved something of a challenge. When the tour was being arranged, a clerk at the Ministry of Information had sent a telegram saying, 'Christmas comes in July' and was reprimanded for sending a message in code. Three other staff were appointed at Denman, and there was of course William Blackwell, who continued his work in the grounds.

Following a strenuous summer of preparation the college was finally opened on 24 September by Sir Richard Livingstone. Guests of honour were of course Lady Denman, Lady Albemarle and Lady Brunner. Alongside them were 250 guests plus the press and the BBC. Tea, provided on this occasion by an outside caterer to relieve the pressure on the college staff, proved too much for the caterer's organisational skills, so Lady Brunner, Joan Yeo and another member of the executive, Dora Tomkinson, donned aprons and set to work serving the visitors. It must have been a huge relief to see the coaches roll out of the grounds and for the resident staff to begin organising dinner for the forty-three guests who were staying to attend the first course to be run at the college. After dinner there was a talk by Dr Adams, an old friend of Grace Hadow, who was head of the National Council for Social Services and who spoke mostly about poetry. After that there was a piano recital by Margaret Deneke, sister of Helena, who subsequently often came to entertain at the college. She freely admitted that she lost all sense of time when playing so it was the job of her chauffeur Arthur to come into the recital and ask her to stop playing at the agreed time.

These first students were closely followed by students on a five-day course, 'Country Housewives', which aimed to mix practical skills with a judicious amount of cultural studies. This was an 'A' course, funded by students themselves or their branches, as opposed to 'B' courses, which were funded by the county organisation on condition that the person being trained would pass on their knowledge to other members of the federation. Both kinds of course cost fifteen shillings a night, which included full board and tuition costs. To be sure of filling the college for the first three months all the courses were 'B' courses. One of the reasons for fixing the length of the course was that you had to provide food rationing coupons for a stay of more than five days, but it was also felt that any greater length of time away from home might alienate the family who were having to cope without their mainstay.

Everyone coming to Denman was greeted not only by Betty Christmas but also by her dog, Sam, a black Labrador given to her by Lady Brunner. This dog, as Jane Robinson puts it in her book *A Force to be Reckoned With*, 'stank to high heaven'. He also thought himself the leader of the pack, as he slept on any bed he chose where the bedroom door had been left open. For people who liked domestic dogs this may not have mattered but many, particularly farming people whose dogs would have known their place, must have smiled through gritted teeth and muttered among themselves while making very sure their bedroom doors were firmly closed to intruders.

Betty Christmas was diagnosed with cancer in 1951 and was ill for the next five years until she died in 1956 at the age of forty-six. During this time she refused to give up her work, so the other staff shielded her from much of the day-to-day administration. She was mourned by everyone who knew her and, as one member of the college staff said of her, 'Wherever Miss Christmas was, there was laughter'.

It took a while to find a replacement for Betty Christmas and for two years Denman was without a warden. Eventually Cecily McCall was given the job. She had had an interesting career, being at one point, as I have already said, organiser to the education subcommittee, but in 1945 she had been dismissed from this post by Lady Denman when she decided to stand for Parliament as a Labour candidate. The daughter of a barrister, she was an intelligent and forceful personality who had had an eventful career at Oxford University. She had been rusticated – sent down – at one point for staying out all night and when restored to residence at her college had failed her final exam. Not a propitious start in life! She had, however, a great deal of energy and was full of ideas, not always, it has to be said, very carefully thought through. After failing to become an MP she had returned to Norfolk to work in a hospital and was now in her mid-fifties with a house, two poodles, three geese and a garden to care for. The lure of Denman, which she had been involved with from the start, led her to give up these commitments and move to Berkshire as it then was. (It is now part of Oxfordshire.)

Once there, her immediate task was to get to grips with the financial situation, which was not a healthy one. Not for the first time, by the end of 1956 there was an excess of expenditure over income of more than £3,000, which was made up by a grant from the national executive, but the national treasurer, Mrs Methuen, felt this continual running at a loss should not continue. The college must be made to pay its way.

Cecily McCall decided that the restriction on branches visiting the college, which had been limited to two weeks in the summer, should be extended and people should be able to come at any time of the year. She argued that people would not want to come to the college if they knew little about it so this was one way of stimulating interest in the courses they ran. It of course made a great deal of extra work for the staff, who resented the extra cleaning incurred when so many extra feet were tramping through the house. Not to mention the cups of tea that had to be made to send visitors on their way in happy mood. As there was now a new dining room and a dishwasher, students didn't have to help with the washing up, so Cecily decided the college could perfectly well cater for day students. She instigated new courses – one for mothers and babies which caused a lot of anxiety beforehand, though the mothers thought it was wonderful and the staff found it not as stressful as they had expected. She organised a family week in August where children would camp in the grounds and between these two events organised a flower show which, when advertised in *Home and Country*, attracted some 4,000 WI members in coaches, which had to pass through the narrow lanes of Marcham.

Cecily was full of good ideas and good intent. She was energetic and innovative, but she was not Betty Christmas, and not only was she not Betty Christmas, she had given away Sam, Betty's beloved Labrador. It was all too much. The secretary, the bursar and the housekeeper resigned. It is not uncommon when there is a new head of an organisation for people who have been happy working under the old head to resign. It is accepted that this will happen and that the new person in charge will employ other people who will fit in to the new system. Unfortunately Cecily did not have the opportunity to appoint new people. She was asked to resign by the national executive. At first she refused to go, and one can see why. She had been brought in to increase the appeal of the courses being run and had taken steps to involve a wider tranche of the membership, all with the aim of making the college pay its way, which she had done. The strain of all this activity, and perhaps a lack of consultation with the staff, meant that she failed to carry the staff with her. It may well be that her left-wing views and the vigour with which she pursued everything she did also frightened the rather more conservative-minded executive. At any rate, she had left the college in 1958, after less than two years in the post, to the relief of some people, if not all.

For some months the college was without a warden, but in 1959 Marjorie Moller was appointed. Miss Moller, aged sixty, had just retired as head of Headington School for Girls, a large private school in one of the outlying suburbs of Oxford. With a new director of studies, Hilda Jones, and a new housekeeper, Nora Lewis, the college had a full complement of senior staff and it was felt that Denman could now settle down and concentrate on what it did best: providing a high standard of education.

There was still, however, the money problem. By 1960, however, it was decided to dedicate the fundraising in that year to raising a fund for Denman so it could finally become financially viable. Miss Moller modified Cecily McCall's decision to allow visitors at any time of year and suggested it would be better if branch visits could be between March and November. While continuing the mother and baby sessions, she got rid of the family camping. The appeal to the branches in 1960 brought in far more than their aim of £25,000. They actually raised £39,243. So the future seemed secure.

The college has always put on a great variety of courses and it is interesting to track the changes in demand for them over the years. In 1949 there were no craft appreciation courses, no practical art or craft classes, no sport and leisure, no personal development, no flower arranging and naturally nothing on video, photography or TV. There were, however, a great many – fourteen – on gardening and the countryside, food and drink, social studies/ history, and there were thirty-one for country housewives. By 1996 there were no courses for country housewives or domestic subjects, but there were fourteen on practical craft and nine on practical art, many fewer on gardening and social studies though double the number of courses on singing and music. In 2013 the courses covered a staggering number of topics, ranging from cryptic crosswords to courses entitled Know Your Computer, alongside Crochet for Beginners, Creative Paper Cutting, Taking Oral Histories, and Complementary Therapies, to name but a few. As Anne Stamper, the WI archivist, says, 'Generally speaking, the more serious "lecture courses" have declined in favour of more active participatory courses. Perhaps we can all get "culture" through some of the television programmes available today that our predecessors did not have.'

In his opening address Sir Richard Livingstone had implied that learning at a high level could only be obtained at the college, whereas in the past it had been undertaken at county level, and therefore it was more readily available to the majority of the membership. All the courses for officer training, which had been held at regional level in the past, were now held at Denman, and all of this leads Maggie Archer in *The Acceptable Face of Feminism* to conclude that Denman was elitist. In reality it seems to me that rather than being elitist, it shows a trend towards centralisation, which was pointed out in the original discussion of the project, and which is probably not a particularly good idea as it gives fewer training opportunities to staff and students than a more diffuse system would.

Funding continued to be a problem. In 1988 there was a drive to raise money for Denman, which would again put it on a sound footing. Much of the womanhood of Derbyshire was to be found that summer ploughing up and down the local swimming baths in sponsored swims. The Derbyshire Federation raised £1,524, much of it in that way. Margaret Dawson of Cartmel wrote, 'I have enjoyed so many courses at Denman that I feel I must send my small donation to the Appeal. No receipt wanted,' she adds thoughtfully and Mary Bowen, who had just won £5 for the letter of the month in *Home and Country*, promptly sent it to the appeal.

The problem of funding Denman continues today, with many of the original concerns raised again in a 2013 survey of members towards Denman. Though members were aware of Denman, only 40 per cent of them had actually visited the college. And the reasons? Too expensive, too far away and the cost of travel was too high. Understandably, people who live near Denman use it more and appreciate what it has to offer. Most people like the historic house and grounds, but when asked if they would be prepared to pay an extra amount on their WI subscription to support Denman, understandably almost 50 per cent said no. The college needs a minimum of sixty members every night, and the price in 2013 to attend a three day jam-making course would be £257, rather a lot of money for many members. The WI intends, however, to set up a 'Friends of Denman' scheme where those who would like to contribute to the college's upkeep can do so.

9

FAMILY PLANNING AND TROUSER
SUITS: 1960–1980

In the late 1950s the Western world was gripped by the fear of nuclear war, with the Campaign for Nuclear Disarmament (CND) being established as a reaction to this in London in 1958. The Cold War rumbled on with occasional confrontations, the most frightening one, between the USA and the USSR, occurring in 1961 – it became known as the Cuban crisis. The WI turned its face away from such difficulties and concentrated on working for peace through fostering peaceful relations between individuals, and noting the widening horizons of their membership.

The 1960s opened up a time for travel abroad. WI membership, like the whole country, fell in love with Italy and Spain, France and Germany. *Home and Country* blazoned this freedom with a cover showing a scene in Italy, while inside the magazine were photographs of WI members on trips to Bavaria and Frejus, in the South of France, while the Mayor of Aberystwyth waved off local members to Florence. Determined to out-travel these commonplace holidaymakers, Lady Haworth wrote an article on her travels to Bokhara, Samarkand and Tashkent. Delegates travelled to Trinidad and Tobago for a conference organised by the Associated Country Women of the World, while travelling in the other direction came Russian visitors to Thriplow WI in Cambridge.

Alongside their courses on patchwork and fabric printing, Denman College supported this zeal for foreign travel by running a course on Spain, while the cookery column, now occupied by a well-known cookery writer of the time, Margaret Ryan, explained how to make pizza, Nuss torte and Spanish omelette.

Meanwhile, underlining their links with philanthropic work in Africa, the eighty-sixth birthday of Dr Albert Schweitzer was celebrated with an account of how Margaret Deneke, member of Elsfield WI and well known for her piano playing at Denman College, had taught Dr Schweitzer English from copies of *Home and Country*, that being the only written English text available on the journey home from Lambarene in West Africa. Dr Schweitzer had established his hospital there in 1913 and it is still a major source of excellence in Gabon, having, according to its website, the lowest incidence of childhood death from malaria in the whole of Africa. A project to establish a farm institute in Karamuja was in the planning stages at federation headquarters, a project which is still ongoing fifty years later.

Developing their interest in house design, which had started in 1951, *Home and Country* was now interested in showing people examples of how old houses had been reconditioned. A resolution from the 1958 conference had awoken members to the fact that 'our domestic architecture is one of our greatest assets'.

The WI was coming to terms with the idea of married women going out to work, particularly to become teachers. There was an acute shortage of primary and secondary school teachers, so an article by someone who had already taken this momentous step was featured in *Home and Country*. It set out a great deal of advice. 'Every married woman returning to teaching should work within easy reach of home, and then only when the youngest child is settled in school. The dangers of farming out young children or helping in any way to add to the growing numbers of "latch key." children are already familiar to most readers.'

A topic that continued to interest members was the use of chemicals, both in food and as used by famers. From a health point of view they were concerned about the effects of fluoridation of the water supply, and they were consulted by the government about their opinions on food additives. The use of toxic sprays, which were being widely used by farmers in the control of pests, both animal and vegetable, with little regard for their impact on the environment and on the food they produced, caused concern, as did the flooding of good agricultural land to provide drinking water for townsfolk. At a countryside conference towards the end of the 1960s attended by Prince Philip, members asked what they could do to help conserve the countryside, their 'green and pleasant land'. They were told they could join in surveys, keep an eye on planning applications, be aware of tree felling and hedgerow destruction and 'be constantly alert to dangers of excessive urbanisation', though the destruction of habitats for wildlife had as much to do with farming techniques as excessive urbanisation.

From a health point of view they were worried about the closure of small hospitals, the lack of provision of professionals such as radiographers and physiotherapists to support the main medical professionals, and they wanted cervical smear tests to be more readily available. They were remarkably prescient in their attitude to cigarette smoking. In 1964, worried about the effect of smoking on young people, they asked the government to restrict smoking in public places such as the tops of buses, cafés, restaurants and on television, a goal which was to take a long time to be attained. The rise in the number of cars on the road was a worry that led to the creation of the Tufty Club, formed to help children learn about road safety with the help of Tufty the Squirrel. *The Furry Folk on Holiday*, a film featuring the intrepid squirrel, got a very good write-up in *Home and Country* with an accompanying photograph of young children enthralled by the antics on the screen. Ernest Marples, Minister for Transport, suggested that the WI should get involved with helping children towards their cycling proficiency test, though he mischievously said he had heard 'scepticism expressed about their suitability for the job'. One WI husband wrote suggesting that the public should be educated so that motoring offences would be treated more seriously.

While the era has been labelled the 'swinging sixties', for most people there wasn't much swinging being done. The majority of women got on with earning a living, feeding the children and pottering about in the garden. Clothes for women were still quite formal, with gloves and matching handbags being the norm and trousers just not available for women. It was only towards the end of the sixties that trouser suits began to come into fashion, and designs by the likes of Hardy Amies and Norman Hartnell featured in *Home and Country* made the idea of wearing trousers attractive. The swinging was done largely by people in the fashion and pop music industries, and it was only in the 1970s that long hair and flared trousers for men and everything tie-dyed for women came into fashion. The bra had not yet been thrown aside, and underpinning the neat skirt and blouse of the working woman might have lurked the Kudly Form, advertised in *Home and Country* as having 'no bones, no hooks, no zips'.

The 1960s began with a welcome reversal of the tide of American pop music, turned back by the Beatles, whose style at first owed everything to Elvis and other pop idols of the time. Indeed, Little Richard shared a residency for several months with the Beatles in Hamburg and taught them how to sing his songs.

Along with the pop music came the use of illicit drugs, and an expression of concern about their circulation made its way into the resolutions for the 1966 AGM. *Home and Country* carried an article about these, trying to put the matter into some sort of perspective by pointing out that most people were dependent on drugs to some extent – aspirins, cigarettes or even tea – then went on to answer the questions: why do people take drugs, where do they get them and how can I spot drug-taking? A thorough description of drugs commonly in use followed. No-one who read the magazine could be in any doubt about what the drugs were or how they affected the user.

American food obtained a foothold in Britain with the establishment of the first Kentucky Fried Chicken outlet in 1964, with Macdonald's and Pizza Hut following ten years later. Meanwhile the WI published a book entitled *The Countrywoman's Year*. It is a curious compilation of old-fashioned ideas and antiquated language. Rather than being a real – or even an idealised – record of how women in the country spent their time, it was a strange mixture of ideas culled from the past, with many of them seemingly based on how a country house was run at the turn of the century. The best room in the house is called the parlour; recipes are called receipts. You are told how to make turtle soup, using only the best sundried turtle meat, of course, which you soak for three to four days, then simmer for eight to ten hours. (No quantity of water is given for this simmering.) Having made her turtle soup, the happy countrywoman then goes on to refurbish the parlour, by making lampshades and weaving rugs. In case she has forgotten how to make her own butter, the instructions are here, and also how to make bread and toys for the children at Christmas, embroider Dorset feather stitching, and run up little dresses for a granddaughter or daughter, complete with smocking. She will be caring for her house plants, though if the house is lit by gas we are warned she will have problems with them as few plants can tolerate even small amounts of gas. Having spruced up her parlour, she may then feel like turning her attention to preparing her home-grown vegetables and fruit for the WI market stall and boiling up a few tons of strawberries for jam, to stock the shelves of her larder. Oh, and she could also make metheglin – not a prescription drug, but a flavoured mead. Three recipes for this, one using sixteen pounds of honey and three gallons of water. There is none of the 'dreary sameness that threatens a semi-urban life'. One can't help thinking that the exhausted countrywoman, subjected to this kind of experience, would have been only too happy to opt for the dreary sameness of a semi-urban life, whatever that is. It was published in 1960, only four years before Terence Conran opened his daring new interior design shop, Habitat, and if this book was an example of the latest thinking in the WI, then the organisation was doomed! Fortunately, it wasn't.

Women's place in society was still in most ways not on an equal footing with that of men. They were still being paid less than men in industry, though not in the professions. This was soon to change thanks to the machinists at the Ford Dagenham plant. In 1968 the machinists, who made covers for car seats, were regraded as

Category B workers, which meant that they were unskilled, which justified the company in paying them 15 per cent less than the men, who were categorised as Category C. This led to a strike by the women, who argued that their work was not unskilled but was semi-skilled. Their strike brought the whole factory to a standstill then spread to other branches of the Ford works. The matter was only resolved when an intervention by Barbara Castle, secretary of state for employment and productivity in Harold Wilson's Labour government, negotiated a rise for the women. Their wages rose so they were only 8 per cent behind the men. Ultimately this action led to the Equal Pay Act of 1970, when women were accorded equal pay with men, an act which came into force in 1975.

One of the major inventions of the decade, or even of the century, for women, was the contraceptive pill. At a stroke it took away the fear of an unwanted pregnancy, which had acted as a severe restraint on young women's behaviour up to that time. Looking back from the present century, the social opprobrium heaped on an unmarried mother seems a ridiculous overreaction. But it was a social disgrace, which resulted in shotgun marriages, or babies born out of wedlock being adopted at birth. Illegitimacy was a severe social stigma for the child, while the mother, sent away if at all possible before the pregnancy began to show, gave birth very often in a home for such disgraced women, only allowed back into the community when the baby had been safely adopted, and her absence was explained by her working away from home, or staying with a relative for a short time. It was meant to be a secret, though it never was, and the woman was branded as a 'loose woman'. For those who managed to marry the father before the baby's birth, it often caused such distress to the girl's parents that it took many years before the girl and her family were reconciled.

The WI approached the topic of contraception with caution. *Home and Country* carried an article called 'A Race with Time' by Margaret Pyke OBE, chairman of the Family Planning Association (FPA). Margaret Pyke was a close friend of Lady Denman. They had worked together from the beginning of the movement, with Lady Denman playing a prominent role both administratively and financially since 1930. The article approached the subject of contraception through worries about the population explosion and the need for there to be enough food in the world to feed its people. There was, said Margaret Pyke, 'a steadily increasing recognition that parents have a right and a duty to plan their families.' There was also the problem of the number of illegal abortions – 50,000 a year – and that was a conservative estimate. She gave a brief history of the FPA, starting with Marie Stopes and describing how in 1921 the windows of her clinic had been smashed and eggs thrown at the people who worked there, how in 1924 the founders of the Manchester clinic had been described in the *Catholic Herald* as 'over-dressed, well fed and badly bred, flaunting cigarettes between their painted lips and shoving birth control down the throats of the unwanted poor'. The Ministry of Health had refused to act, and the assembled moral leadership of the bishops of the Church of England at the Lambeth conference of 1920 had condemned birth control. The tide had begun to turn in the 1950s, however, when to mark the FPA's silver jubilee, the Minister of Health, Iain Macleod, had come out in favour of the movement. Family planning was for married women only, however. A woman had to have an engagement ring firmly on her finger and a date fixed for the wedding before she was allowed to get advice, and it was to be several years before it was available outside marriage.

The 50,000 illegal abortions which caused Margaret Pike so much concern were tackled by Harold Wilson's Labour government in 1967 when the Abortion Act was passed. This meant that a foetus could be aborted before twenty-eight (now twenty-four) weeks' gestation, providing medical practitioners agreed. While in theory an abortion should be carried out only to safeguard the mother's life or mental well-being, in fact many doctors consider that to continue a pregnancy to term will always be more dangerous than an early termination, so the act can be interpreted as 'abortion on demand'. Because of the opposition of many people of the Christian faith, especially Catholics, to abortion, this was not a subject that could be discussed by the WI, with its embargo on topics which might prove divisive. There was, however, a resolution adopted for the 1967 AGM which asked for a change of rule about non-party politics. 'In view of the interest taken in current problems by our members,' it said, they requested that the part of the constitution which stated 'No sectarian or party political matters shall be brought forward for discussion at an Institute meeting' should be replaced by 'No Institute shall be used for purposes of party-political or sectarian propaganda.'

A further freeing up of social rules, or abandoning of principles, depending on your point of view, was the relaxing of the grounds for divorce brought in again by the Wilson government in 1969. Since 1857 the Matrimonial Causes Act had allowed women to divorce their husbands on the grounds of adultery, providing there were other faults such as cruelty, rape or incest. Even then it was an expensive business. This was modified in 1923, when women could divorce on the grounds of adultery only, though this had to be proved. The Divorce Reform Act of 1969 allowed divorce on the ground of irretrievable breakdown of marriage, demonstrated by a period of two years' separation, if both parties agreed to it, and five years if only one of the couple wanted a divorce. Financially, women were worse off after a divorce because the less-wealthy spouse, usually the woman, was awarded money from her husband according to need. This was changed in 1996, when any assets accrued by the couple were split more fairly, which recognised the contribution to the financial welfare of the couple by the homemaker. In 1968, in the lead up to the new divorce act, the WI tabled a resolution at conference about the financial position of divorced women. They felt that provision should be made for the deserted wife for financial security, tax reliefs and pension rights. The number of divorces, which had been 2.6 per 1,000 married people in 1951, rose sharply after the Act and in 1988 was 12.8 per 1,000.

The beginning of the 1960s had seen the rise of the playgroup movement, which provided a support group for mothers and play opportunities for their young children. Many of the mothers, and occasionally fathers, who were involved with the movement were unqualified in the education of young children, and learned on the job. This was just the kind of area of expertise which a place such as Denman College could supply and by 1968 they were advertising courses on 'Starting a playgroup.' Lady Brunner and her husband Sir Felix proved as generous as Lady Denman had been in the past, and gave a craft room to Denman, a facility which was very much appreciated. The queen mother herself opened the new teaching blocks at Denman, which resulted in a whole lot of photographs of the event in *Home and Country*. In 1977 the magazine ran an article on 'Running a playgroup'.

The 1970s

The 1970s saw the rise and increasing importance of the environmental movement. The two international organisations, Friends of the Earth and Greenpeace, both emerged from the anti-nuclear lobby, FOE in the United States, and Greenpeace in Vancouver, Canada. They were formed in the late sixties and arrived here shortly afterwards. Anxieties about the state of the environment raise their heads in the letters pages of *Home and Country*, with concern being expressed about factory farming, the dangers of using fruit sprayed with chemicals for jam-making, and outrage from a reader in the Isle of Wight that the road verges, which had been full of wild flowers, had been mown by the local authority to tidy it up before a visit from the queen. There were also letters about the horror of wearing fur on clothing and the unpleasant realities of factory farming. In the November 1970 edition there were six whole pages given over to how the WI was tackling conservation, with pictures showing members clearing a river (a shallow one, no danger of drowning!), clearing footpaths and planting trees, shrubs and flowers.

The following year, among resolutions for the AGM which included urging the government to stop the closure of rural post offices and to build a third London airport at Foulness, on the Essex coast rather than Cublington, seven miles north of Aylesbury, was a request for the government to hasten research into developing disintegrating plastic packaging.

Dutch Elm disease arrived in 1971, killing the elm trees that had been such an integral part of the British countryside and at a stroke taking away the justification for Elsfield's banner, so carefully worked in 1920 by May Allam and Susan Buchan. By this time, however, the Elsfield branch of the WI was no longer in existence, having closed in 1963 when no-one could be found to take on the job of president.

Sir Eric Ashby, head of the Royal Commission on Environmental Pollution, spoke to the WI about the success of the Clean Air Act and the importance of recycling. The commission continued its work until 2011, when the then government closed it as a money-saving measure.

By 1976 the WI was again discussing pollution, this time water pollution. The WI had been asked to read and comment on the 1974 Control of Pollution Act, which had put restrictions on what could and could not be discharged into waterways and sewers. This act imposed a fine of £20,000 on anyone who broke the provisions of the act. Water authorities for the first time were allowed to disclose what pollutants were going into the rivers. Up to that time, according to *Home and Country*, they had not been allowed to do this because of the importance of not disclosing the formulae used by certain industrial processes and the dangers of industrial espionage. The act also applied to the discharge of nitrates into rivers and streams by farmers.

There seems to have been quite a body of opinion within the WI against nuclear power and for natural energy sources, but resolutions framed around this topic for the AGM in 1976 were never chosen by the executive as being suitable for debate. Nor did resolutions concerning the media and their distorted or sensational presentation of the news and condemnation of rape scenes in television drama. West Sussex was concerned about the invasion of privacy by TV, radio and the press. This wasn't brought to the AGM either. The topics that did make it on to the agenda were rather less controversial, and included flexible transport schemes,

VAT on domestic appliances and keeping the age of consent for sex at sixteen. Nothing there to rock the boat!

The following year there was a plethora of resolutions about water conservation, because 1976 had been a year of glorious sunshine, which meant that there had been water shortages. Guernsey put in a resolution pleading for the government to veto any more fast-breeder reactors, but this again never made it to the AGM, and once again Ideford and Luton in Devon wanted research into renewable energy, a plea which was ignored.

Edward Heath, Prime Minister from 1970 to 1974, presided over dramatic changes in the social life of the country. He brought in boundary changes to local government areas that had remained unchanged since Anglo-Saxon times. The Minister for Local Government asked the WI to comment on the boundary changes and for their ideas on possible names for metropolitan areas, ways to protect local identities and to ensure that the special interest of rural areas was not overshadowed by the changes. Chunks of what had been Berkshire and Buckinghamshire now found themselves in Oxfordshire, and changes such as this were replicated throughout the land, so the WI's advice on preserving local identity would be useful.

The changes in county boundaries also affected which federation WI branches belonged to. It was decided at national level that federations would conform to the new boundaries but it took several years to implement the changes, a process not completed until 1982. Yorkshire was the last county federation to comply, and then not without a struggle. The national executive only learned via the *Yorkshire Post* that the Yorkshire executive intended to ask all its 22,000 members in 620 branches what they wanted to do. The fact that the very large Yorkshire Federation had not even informed the national executive of their decision, and that they did not intend to comply with the regulations laid down by the national executive, must have raised the spectre of disintegration of the entire structure to Anne Harris, the then president. This was not the way our movement worked, she thundered. One part of our organisation could not decide to take a different line from the rest. The rebellion was quashed and the recalcitrant Yorkshire executive brought into line.

The coinage changed somewhat earlier than the boundary changes, in 1971, when Britain lost the pounds, shillings, and pence and acquired merely pounds and pence, at a stroke simplifying the arithmetic taught in primary schools and putting up prices, since the conversion from one system to another invariably meant a rounding up of the cost of an item. Well, that was the public perception, at any rate. There is little trace of this in *Home and Country*.

Similarly, the dreadful situation in Northern Ireland with the activities of the IRA and the official response to them, the massacre of Bloody Sunday in 1972, the bombing of a pub in Birmingham in 1976 and at the end of the decade the murder of Lord Mountbatten, did not feature in the WI magazine.

Nor did 'battered wives'. The phrase makes them sound like the product of a fish-and-chip shop, but it was and remains no laughing matter. Violence within marriage was a worry long before the twentieth century. In 1878 Frances Power Cobbe had published a pamphlet entitled 'Wife Torture in England', and the subject of Anne Bronte's novel *The Tenant of Wildfell Hall* was a marriage between a drunken husband and his wife, whom he abused. The subject dropped out of public awareness in the first half of the twentieth century but came to the fore again in the

1970s, when Erin Pizzey founded the Chiswick Women's Refuge in 1971. The 1976 Domestic Violence and Matrimonial Proceedings Act made it easier for women to obtain an injunction, now known as a restraining order, to try to prevent husbands from perpetrating violence on their partners, and by 1981, some 1,000 women and 1,700 children were being accommodated in 200 refuges throughout the country.

The decade saw the rise of the new feminist movement, which may have seemed to the general public very remote from what the WI stood for and must certainly have appeared so for the majority of its members. However, the difference between the new feminists and the WI was more like the difference between the suffragists and the suffragettes. The suffragists were horrified at the violence of the suffragettes, though acknowledging in the long run their effectiveness. The feminist movement was working for the freeing up of women from their traditional role within the family and seeking a wider and more fulfilling life for them, to some extent what the WI had been aiming for in a quieter way for many years. However, according to Maggie Andrews, the new feminism relied on the belief that political action was the way forward, which immediately made a difficulty for the WI. Their constitution said they should not get involved in party politics, but this was sometimes interpreted as taking no political action at all. The new feminists made a fuss, and so were taken very seriously indeed by the establishment of the time, not so much because of their ideas but because of their nuisance value. One of the key texts for the movement was Germaine Greer's *The Female Eunuch*, published in 1970, in which Greer propounded the idea that the traditional suburban consumerist nuclear family represses women sexually, which devitalises them. Little wonder the WI, valuing as it did the role of women as carers of children and old people, should turn its back on such views. But turning its back on the new feminists meant that the WI became for many women an irrelevance. Why join an organisation that never dealt with the challenges facing young women? Numbers began to fall and recruitment suddenly took on a new urgency, with WI numbers dropping from 467,000 in 1954 to 272,503 in 1995.

The 1960s and 1970s were a time of great change in many women's lives. Work opportunities had opened up, co-habitation rather than marriage had increased enormously, the stigma of bastardy had been removed and by 1976 women had been awarded equal pay for equal work. In theory, anyway. One big drawback of this situation, which had improved in so many ways, was that, as Jane Lewis in *Women in Britain since 1945* points out, 'While women have undoubtedly increased their paid employment, there is little sign that they have significantly diminished their unpaid housework and child care and they may well have increased their unpaid work in caring for the elderly.' This was another factor which was bound to have an effect on WI membership. When a woman has worked all day, done the housework when she gets home, and finally put the children to bed, there is little time or energy for going out to an evening meeting.

10

MARGARET THATCHER AND PRINCESS DIANA: 1980–2000

Reading copies of *Home and Country* from the 1980s and 1990s and remembering what the country was concerned about gave me the impression that the WI was living in a parallel universe to mainstream history. In a way, they were. The 1980s was the decade of Margaret Thatcher, the first woman Prime Minister the country had ever had and therefore, one would have thought, a topic of comment for the WI. There is no mention of her until 1991, when she had been ousted from power in what one might call a palace coup, engineered in no small part by Geoffrey Howe, of whom the Labour politician Denis Healey had once memorably said that being attacked by him was like being savaged by a dead sheep.

The reason for her lack of presence in the pages of *Home and Country* may well be that she broke the consensus about the direction the country should be travelling in. From 1945, whichever party was in power, the feeling was that capitalism, which had brought enormous benefits to the country, should have some sort of control exerted over it, to curb its worst excesses. The curbs had been applied by the unions, representing the working classes, and for the system to work well, there had to be a balance between the interests of capitalism and those of the working classes. In the 1970s the unions had, many people thought, become too powerful. They were largely on the side of working men and had little thought and even less respect for the women in their ranks. In areas such as South Yorkshire, where the male-dominated industries of mining and engineering were placed, the position taken by the National Union of Mineworkers under the union boss Arthur Scargill was an extreme one.

Union action brought down the Heath government and when Margaret Thatcher came to power she was determined to deal with the unions once and for all. She did this very successfully by engineering a confrontation with the miners over mine closures. Having destroyed one side of the balance of power, the unions, capitalism ran amok. Services which had been taken into state control in the wake of the Second World War – services such as electricity, water and the railways – were denationalised and sold off. Abolition of fixed commissions in the London stock market enabled British firms to take over existing brokering and jobbing houses in the City and to create enormous banking conglomerates, which in turn led to a class of super-rich bankers. 'There is no such thing as society', Mrs Thatcher is alleged to have said, and 'Greed is good' became a watchword. 'Loadsamoney', a term coined by Harry Enfield and intended to be satirical, lost its satirical edge and was taken up by many of the rich young bankers as a watchword to live by.

While the hearts of many WI members must have warmed to Margaret Thatcher, many did not. She was one of the most divisive politicians in recent times, and party political at that. Mrs Thatcher believed that anyone who was not for her was against her. And she politicised almost very aspect of society. 'Are they one of us?' she is reputed to have asked. Being an inclusive organisation this was the very antithesis of what the WI meant and there were consequently great swathes of public life that could not be discussed in the pages of *Home and Country* because of its political implications.

Fortunately there were some areas of life the magazine could comment on and the national executive could act on. The NFWI had been a founder member of the 300 Club when it formed in 1980. Then there were only nineteen women in Parliament and *Home and Country* carried an article by Lesley Abdela, a Labour MP, about the need for more women MPs, preferably half the parliamentary intake. The title of the group came from the fact that there were 635 MPs, half of which would be 317 and a half. You couldn't have a group called 'The three hundred and seventeen and a half club' so they settled for the snappier title of '300 Club'.

There was also royalty, a popular favourite with any women's magazine. The wedding of Prince Charles and Diana Spencer triggered an article about wedding dresses. In 1992, too, the February issue of *Home and Country* carried a photograph of Princess Diana. She had lunch with representatives of the WI to celebrate them having raised £401,162 for various children's charities. Princess Diana wowed the WI, as she did most people who met her. 'She was so natural, such fun to be with,' said one member of the national executive. The meal provided consisted of Parma ham and melon, salmon supreme in champagne sauce, new potatoes and a 'frou-frou' of vegetables. Princess Di, however, nibbled on a small serving of vegetables and drank nothing but water. 'Does the Princess always eat so little?' asked one woman. 'Oh no, she has a very healthy appetite,' the private secretary answered, 'but obviously someone in her position needs to talk rather than eat at such functions.' Astonishingly there is nothing in *Home and Country* about her very sad death in August 1997. Considering what distress was shown by the public at that time, I find it bizarre that there is no obituary, no warm recollections, nothing at all about that dreadful car crash and the princess's subsequent death. I can only infer that the editorial board was out of sympathy with Diana, and disliked the way she dealt with her husband's infidelity and her way of dealing with the media, which they may have felt brought the monarchy into disrepute.

During the eighties the WI could and did continue its interest in countries overseas. December 1981 brought Christmas greetings from Lesotho, and news about the NFWI project in Zimbabwe and Lesotho. The 'Women and Water' appeal, run in conjunction with UNICEF, had installed 430 water supply systems and 210 water minders had been trained, sixty of them women. It was not, unfortunately, cutting down on gastro-intestinal problems or typhoid because of contamination between collecting and using the water, and poor hygiene was blamed. The following year brought news that with the aid of a better water supply women were able to grow their own vegetables, which had previously been imported from South Africa and were therefore expensive. By 1985, with a target of £20,000 for bringing water to the villages, they had in fact raised £50,836, with latrines now included in the aims of the project. Many of the women in Britain who had contributed to this scheme would have remembered just how difficult life was without a proper water supply. No wonder they exceeded their target.

An interest in world affairs took a WI delegate to the Second International Interdisciplinary Congress on Women to discuss women's lack of power and how to gain it. She also went to hear about wife beating, which was legal in Kenya, and how the women in Algeria were not allowed to form organisations and were imprisoned if they did, though they couldn't be brought to trial because there was no law under which they could be tried. The congress also discussed dowry burning in India, a situation where a bride is bullied by her husband and in-laws to such an extent that she will commit suicide when the dowry is considered insufficient, so freeing up the husband to remarry. Female circumcision, now called Female Genital Mutilation (FGM) was also on the agenda. As one French doctor commented, it was 'time that respect for culture gave way to respect for women'.

Conflict in the world made its way into *Home and Country* only very indirectly, and usually later than the event. The Falklands War, waged against Argentina in 1982, was unremarked at the time. These islands in the South Atlantic had been invaded by the Argentinians and the invasion was contested by the British, who had settled the islands from the mid-nineteenth century onwards. Although the war did not last very long – seventy-four days from April to June – there were 649 Argentinians killed, 255 British and three Falkland islanders. There were also a number of wounded, and on the first anniversary of the ending of the war *Home and Country* carried an article saying it was important not to hide away the wounded, but for them to take an active part in society so their sacrifice could be honoured and their lives made more meaningful. There was also an article about the working lives of three women farmers in the islands.

The first Gulf War, too, waged in Kuwait, only found its way into the magazine via a mention in an editorial in October 1990, when the war had started in August of that year. The editorial complained about the difficulty of keeping the price of the magazine down because of the Gulf War and the high interest rates. 'These days a Gulf war threatens and interest rates remain so high that everyone – our advertisers included – is cutting back on spending.' A curious coupling of events.

While *Home and Country* obviously found it difficult to comment on wars, one might have thought the opposite of that – the peace movement – might have elicited some comment. One omission from the record of events is any mention of a topic which was dear to many women's hearts in the 1980s, Greenham Common, where a peace camp had been established. This was an RAF site housing American nuclear weapons, and the inhabitants of the camp monitored what was happening at the base. In 1982, some 30,000 women encircled the base in order to draw attention to the presence of American missiles on British soil and to try to influence the government to order the Americans to withdraw them. In 1983 an even larger contingent, 70,000 women, formed a fourteen-mile human chain from Greenham to Aldermaston. It was not until 1991 that the missiles were removed, and a token camp remained until the year 2000 to establish a monument to the event, though this suffered so much vandalism that it was eventually removed.

Although the WI did not involve itself in any way with Greenham, there is one letter in *Home and Country* which shows how WI members felt about the peace movement at this time. The *Sunday Telegraph* seems, in an astonishing slip of the pen or typewriter, to have linked the WI with the Campaign for Nuclear Disarmament (CND). A lady from Woolverstone near Ipswich wrote that although she found this mistake quite incredible, she was appalled that apparently countless members were horrified by it, as if CND were an unspeakable organisation campaigning to set the word alight. 'Certainly we should protest strongly at our misrepresentation by the Press,' she writes, 'but instead of being shocked, we should have been proud that it was thought that women would be behind such a humanitarian campaign. I only regret that it isn't.'

Admittedly many people who went to Greenham were left-wing, but if WI members were as shocked as this letter states, then the WI at this time consisted of a great many members who were conservative with a small 'c' and very likely Conservative with a large 'C'. It's ironic that the WI, which had so many pacifist Quakers among its members in the 1930s that they felt unable to take part in any activity which overtly supported the war effort in 1939, were appalled to find themselves aligned with CND which, being an anti-war group, also had a large number of Quaker members.

With so much of the country's life being beyond the pale, there was little of serious import to discuss. One exception at the end of the 1980s was a very short item on child sexual abuse when it was noted that Rolf Harris had made a short film, *Kids Can Say No*, which might help adults to talk to children about a difficult subject.

Sport, food, consumerism and recruiting new members took precedence in the 1980s. WI members were shown at a hockey camp, sky jumping, shooting, sailing and swimming. But what hit the headlines in *Home and Country* was the tennis tournament when the finals were held at the Queen's Club in London. Some 1,120 people entered the competition, which was in its ninth year, and the Lawn Tennis Association very kindly waived their fee, which was just as well, since it was the first time the championship had failed to attract sponsorship.

There were various issues about food and cooking. There was an article rhapsodising about microwave ovens, eulogised as more a friend than a gadget, and the cookery column was now concerned with calorie counting, a sign that body image had moved up the social agenda. The importance of labelling food accurately and in detail was stressed by Caroline Walker, a nutritionist, who insisted that people should know just what was contained in the food they bought – how much sugar, how much salt and how much fibre. A resolution for the 1986 AGM was a request that Crown Immunity should be removed from hospital kitchens so they could be inspected under the Health and Safety at Work Act. This was withdrawn when the government agreed to include this in the Health and Food Act of 1984, which was already on the statute book. The WI in this case, as in others at this time, was timid in its approach and was certainly not in the game of pressurising the government in any way, something of a disappointment when they could have taken such a lead.

The importance of not being overweight was highlighted when Wales decided collectively to lose weight. The Health Promotion Authority of Wales in conjunction with the Welsh WI aimed for Welsh WI members to lose 2,550 stones – the weight of two double-decker buses. The Wales way to healthy eating featured a lamb and leek stir-fry.

Members and the national executive were well aware that they needed to recruit younger members. In 1983 they decided to promote the WI through a variety of means. They aimed to stimulate public awareness, to 'put our house in order' and to improve what they offered.

They decided that the promotion would home in on three specific issues: women in public life, women in education and women and health. The upshot of this was an article in *Home and Country* by Baroness Lockwood, who had just finished an eight-year stint as first chair of the Equal Opportunities Commission; a WI bus which toured the southern counties with a travelling exhibition entitled 'Women in the Community'; and the manufacture and promotion of a sweatshirt bearing the WI logo modelled by a very glamorous member of the sales and promotion subcommittee. Meanwhile, as a demonstration of what could be done to raise the profile of individual branches, Totnes WI decorated and manned – or rather 'womanned' – a float entitled 'Jam Tomorrow' in their local carnival. Elizabeth Pullin from Steeple Ashton in Wiltshire, however, had a different take on the problem. She wrote suggesting that the WI should oppose cuts to the NHS and went on, 'One way of trying to recruit younger members would be to concern ourselves more with current events and make people realize we are something more than a lot of middle-aged ladies making jam.'

'Scene 80' was a dramatic way of bringing the WI to public notice and must have taken a great deal of energy to organise both at national and county level. Patron of the event was the actor Donald Sinden, and the event was sponsored by Johnsons Wax. Several county federations put on an entertainment: at Salisbury a miscellany of different acts, among them 'While Cerne Sleeps', the life of the village of Cerne Abbas traced though the centuries, and Sonning Glebe's contribution, a dance drama – 'Jabberwocky'. There were performances in Newcastle, Horsham, Preston, Taunton, Mold and Colchester, all put together and presented by individual county federations. Whether these performances were enjoyed by people outside the WI is not recorded, but it doesn't seem to have helped with recruiting new members.

The approach to recruitment in the 1980s not having been a notable success, in the nineties a different approach was attempted. The nineties were the years of sponsorship and marketing. 1990 alone saw the final of the NatWest choir of the year, Baxter's 'Back to British Food' competition, Calor Gas's 'Citizen of the Year' award and a Vauxhall-sponsored 'Driver of the Year' competition. Bridgemere Gardens sponsored the WI entry in the Chelsea Flower Show and the Marmalade competition sponsored by Silver Spoon was won by Pat Hayward of Caton WI with her marrow and orange marmalade.

The chairman of the WI at that time had obviously absorbed the marketing ethos with a vengeance. In her column she likened the WI to a shop and pointed out the importance of having a 'product' which was marketable and attractive. She urged branch members to see what spice they could add and ensure they were offering an attractive buy. 'We need all the purchasers we can get to ensure that our organization will always command the prime spot on the shelf and that the public will like what they see, continue to buy and keep our cash flow healthy.'

So protracted is the metaphor and so far from the ideals of the WI when it was first set up that I was unsure at first what she was writing about. I think that column would have been a great disappointment to Grace Hadow, who had set up an organisation which she hoped would help build a better Britain. That it should be reduced to crude marketing language such as this would have been a blow.

The major concern of the nineties being the recruitment of new young members, the WI decided to approach the problem from a consumerist point of view. In 1995 they obtained a grant from the Chartered Institute of Marketing Charitable Trust to develop the role of marketing in the WI. One result was a booklet entitled *How to Have a Successful WI*, which largely encapsulates the executives' preoccupation with attracting new membership, in particular younger women. This contains many useful suggestions and ideas of how to rejuvenate an elderly branch, unfortunately couched in language that some would find uncongenial. According to the booklet, there are five things to be taken into account when running a branch of the WI: Product, Price, Place, Promotion and People. The people is obviously the people you meet at the meetings, the place is where the branch meets and the product is what members get out of belonging to a branch: the monthly meeting, any groups they might attend, the friendship, the learning. The price is equally obviously what you pay for belonging. The booklet describes the cost of joining as 'incredibly inexpensive'. Well, perhaps, though your idea of 'incredibly inexpensive' may be rather different from a marketing person's idea of 'inexpensive' if you are a young mother with a growing family supported by a hard-pressed husband, or an older woman on a restricted income. And the expense does not stop there. There are the raffles, the coffee mornings, the WI goods for sale. All, of course, for worthy causes, but still a strain on one's purse. It says much for the goodwill the WI engenders that people carry on paying out month after month. The best part of the booklet is about Promotion – how the WI sells itself – and as I have commented earlier, the WI can be very inward-looking. There follow some excellent ideas on promoting the WI, involving members in decision making and extracting ideas from them about where they want their branch to go.

As the 1990s progressed the constraints on political discussion imposed by the divisive regime of Mrs Thatcher began to ease up. There were mutterings from the membership that important matters were being ignored. In 1991, for instance, an editorial says, 'A year ago ... one by one the countries of Eastern Europe shook off repressive regimes to embrace democracy.' It goes on to mention the fall of the Berlin Wall, which caused so much excitement among the general public that some people actually went over to Berlin just to be there as this momentous event was taking place. More bloodthirsty was the gruesome fate of President Ceauşescu in Romania, which was watched with such fascination on television. 'Now a year later we are at war with Iraq', writes the chairman, the war in question being the first Gulf War. 'The WI, as a women's organization, is deeply concerned about the suffering of women and children and the elderly, the innocent victims of events, even though we cannot make a national statement about the war as we have been asked to do by some members and the media.' People realised they were living through great historical events and they wanted the WI to articulate their feelings and were disappointed at their focus on events within the organisation. Not surprising, then, that there was a drop in membership of 10,000 in 1991.

As the decade continued, there was more political comment on a variety of topics. In 1995 there was an article about the WIs in Northern Ireland. The lady interviewed said that being on the outskirts of Belfast members were often scared to go out at night to meetings because of the troubles. She blamed the education system and the churches for encouraging sectarianism, but went on, 'Since the 1994 ceasefire terrorism has lessened. There are no bag searches in Marks and Spencer's now and you can go shopping in decent shoes, not trainers.' (People wore trainers so if there were a bomb scare they could run.)

In 1998, *Home and Country* carried an article about life for women in Afghanistan at a time before Britain had become embroiled in a war there. It consisted of an interview with Mari, a young woman living in London who had left Kabul two years before when the Taliban had invaded her city, and set up the Islamic Emirate of Afghanistan. Mari outlined the curtailment of freedom for the women of Kabul, pointing out that the burka had only been introduced into the country as recently as 1953. The article raised the profile of a campaign called 'Living Shadows' being run by WomenAid, a humanitarian and aid charity which works for the good of men, women and children throughout the world.

The NFWI had long had a presence in Brussels at the heart of the European Union, having a representative on COFACE – the Confederation of Family Organisations in the European Union – and CEGG – Consumers in the European Community Group. But towards the end of the century there was a somewhat ambivalent attitude towards it. Given the non-party-political stance of the WI, it was astonishing to see in 1999 an article by one Rodney Atkinson, billed as a leading member of the United Kingdom Independence Party (UKIP), suggesting that Britain should withdraw from the EU and return to the common market of self-governing nations. Presumably the editor, and perhaps the general public, did not realise that UKIP was a political party, but thought of them rather as a far-out pressure group.

They certainly began to take notice of more mainstream politics when later that year readers were invited to submit questions to be put to members of the government, the deputy Prime Minister John Prescott, Tessa Jowell, and Estelle Morris. 'In January 2000 Tony Blair will be in the hot seat,' *Home and Country* wrote. Was that a threat or a promise?

II

STITCHING, SELLING AND SAVING THE COUNTRYSIDE: WI LONG-TERM INTERESTS AND ACHIEVEMENTS

There are some topics which don't fit easily into one particular decade – long-term goals and interests which have continued from the beginning of the Women's Institute movement and which are still with us today. Selling produce is one, as are the skills that have been traditionally thought of as the province of women: knitting, crochet, embroidery and sewing. Care of the countryside has also been a major concern that became increasingly important as the twentieth century progressed. They have been an important part of the work of the WI and deserve a chapter to themselves.

WI Markets

From the beginning, one of the aims of the WI was to increase food production, but it was no use increasing the food supply if the food supplied could not reach potential customers. Some device was needed to link the food with the public, and the WI found the solution by setting up markets run by volunteers.

The first market started in Criccieth, North Wales, and was a wholesale rather than a retail outlet. Dorothy Drage was one of the women involved. In the summer of 1916 she started collecting and marketing fruit, vegetables and eggs. Twice a week the WI held a sale, staffed by voluntary workers. Goods were sold wholesale until 4 p.m., after which they were sold to the general public. After three and a half months they had made £250 profit, which was paid back to the producers. 'We took turns in collecting and selling,' Mrs Drage explained, 'and we had anxious moments on several days wondering how much produce was going to come in, and welcomed with joy the larger amounts from the larger gardens and farms.'

Egg distribution was particularly difficult for farmers because marketing them was in the hands of dealers who controlled prices. Colonel Stapleton-Cotton's egg collection service and depot at Llanfairpwll was the first to take distribution out of the hands of the dealers so farmers got a fair price for their eggs. It was he who introduced the idea of grading and testing eggs, and he paid commission on the quantity received.

In 1931 the Ministry of Agriculture discussed with the NFWI the question of setting up markets all over the country. A grant from the Carnegie Trust, of which Lady Denman was a trustee, was obtained to pay the expenses of a marketing organiser and the NFWI set about encouraging the establishment of market stalls. By 1939 there were about a hundred of them. In her slim wartime book succinctly entitled *Women's Institutes*, Cicely McCall tells the story of one egg producer who had just delivered eight dozen eggs at the market, and who then telephoned to say there was one hard-boiled egg among the batch she had left. The market organiser had then to gently shake every egg to find the one which had been boiled. Heaven knows how that had happened!

One of the major difficulties during the Second World War was the sale of eggs. The WI had appointed a marketing organiser in 1932, a Miss Cox, who at the beginning of the war in 1939 met Mr Flatt of the eggs branch of the Ministry of Agriculture to discuss the restrictions on the sale of eggs imposed on the markets. Mr Flatt said that 'under the present order, owners of fifty or less hens may sell direct to consumers, but they are not allowed to supply eggs for sale on WI market stalls'. I think this demonstrates a level of central control of the food supply we would find difficult to tolerate now, and it must have been only the knowledge that their role was vital in the fight against fascism that made conditions such as this tolerable.

Miss Cox's job was to help set up new markets and advise them how to register as provident societies. Each market was run by a marketing committee and if someone wanted to sell their produce, they bought a share in the enterprise, which pre-war cost one shilling and entitled you to sell your goods on the stall. Shares were not limited to WI members. Even men could join! Prices were regulated according to the local current rates and no market was allowed to undercut neighbouring retailers. The producer was paid eleven pence in the shilling, the remaining penny going towards the expense of the stall. The organiser of a market stall was given a small honorarium and her bus fares and the bus fares of the people staffing the stall were usually paid, so they were not out of pocket.

Newbury market had strict rules, which suppliers were expected to adhere to. They were typed on foolscap paper and handed to every contributor to the stall. The rules were very clear and very detailed:

Two invoices clearly made out stating institute, name of sender, quantity of goods sent and exact weight.

Initial any eggs, make sure they are quite clean as otherwise they do not sell well, and please remember that to get the best price no egg should weigh less than two ounces.

All stalks to be removed from lettuce, cabbage etc. and all roots cleaned.

Onions, carrots, turnips when young to be tied in bundles of six, twelve or twenty-four; cabbage plants etc. must be in scores (twenties); cut flowers must be fresh and tied in bunches with the name of the sender attached.

All pots of honey should be labelled with their origin and jams, marmalade, lemon cheese, pickles etc. should carry the name of the maker.

Butter must have net weight written on wrapping paper.

And finally:

No goods can be received after twelve noon, commission will be deducted at 1d in the shilling and all goods are received at owner's risk. Anything not called for by closing time will be sent to the local hospital.

In 1943 when Cicely McCall published her book, *Women's Institutes*, the total turnover for the markets was £30,000. The money earned from selling the produce belonged to the woman who sold her produce, and, as Cicely McCall says, this could have been the first money she had ever had which belonged entirely to her. 'She can buy a pair of new curtains, or a plant for the garden, or a present for Mum, and her conscience is clear that the money is hers to spend extravagantly or wisely as she likes.' By the middle of the war the WI markets, which now numbered 300, had become an important part of the food distribution network.

During the 1930s the stalls sold every kind of home produce – brawn, cakes, cream, butter, eggs, poultry, vegetables, flowers, preserves. One stall even sold shampoo for dogs, as well as for their owners. During the war, however, rationing limited what the stalls could sell. They couldn't sell dairy products or jam. Only a small amount of poultry and only long-established stalls could sell baking, because of the fat and sugar used in them, but they could sell fruit, rabbits and vegetables. It was also sometimes difficult to get goods to market because of the petrol restrictions, but in spite of the difficulties, the number of market stalls increased during the war.

A more up-to-date experience of WI markets is provided by Margaret Strother, who sold cakes and puddings at Ambleside WI during the 1990s. 'The branch was very keen on craft,' says, Margaret,

and I'm useless at that sort of thing, but I do make jam and marmalade and I can make cakes. So I got involved with the market. This was a completely different organization from the branch. It had a separate committee and its own separate organiser. You had to register with the organisation and you had to pay ten percent of your earnings to the WI. I had a baking day on a Thursday and usually made half a dozen sticky toffee puddings and four lemon curd cakes which were very popular. People would buy one one week and ask for another for the following week, so I'd make an extra one then. I also sold marmalade when I'd made some, and sometimes jam, but there didn't seem to be a good source of fruit in the Lake District. Perhaps it was to do with the soil or the climate.

'It rains a lot in the Lake District,' Margaret pointed out.

So the market was not held outside but in the room where we had our WI meetings, the Village Hall. We were open from nine o'clock till twelve, but of course we had to get there earlier to set up the stalls. Other people made considerably more than I did. There were two men who sold vegetables they'd grown in their gardens. And we also had craft stalls – knitting, crochet, sewing, jewellery, bead-work, and one man did wood carving. The craft stalls did well on the run up to Christmas, but we always had quite a lot of tourists who came to buy souvenirs. People would come in on a Friday from the outlying villages to buy at our stall. It was very popular. The craft stalls made their stalls look as attractive as possible but we didn't need to with the cake stall. One woman specialized in fruit cakes and she was very busy before Christmas. Everything sold out straight away. From time to time we'd have a trip round the local shops to see what they were charging. We kept our prices very much in line with them.

Hygiene checks became a nuisance. 'They were introduced during the nineties and gradually got more and more bureaucratic,' said Margaret. 'In the end there was so much paperwork I was glad to give up. The inspection from the WI organiser was very stringent. The cake had to be put in the bag just so, and all the ingredients listed. I could see that it had to be done but it made it a lot more difficult,' she admitted.

Sewing and embroidery

Over the centuries sewing, in particular embroidery, has been closely associated with what it means to be a woman. But some feminists have expressed the view that in a patriarchal society it has also been a means of oppressing women, with a submissive girl bent over her embroidery being seen as the archetype of a good, compliant, well-brought-up girl who would make an excellent wife and mother. In *Pride and Prejudice*, set at the beginning of the nineteenth century, Jane Austen has Mr Bingley describe what he expects of an accomplished woman: 'They all paint tables, cover screens and net purses.' To which his sister adds, 'A woman must have a thorough knowledge of singing, drawing, dancing and the modern languages to deserve the word.' At least Miss Bingley included some physical and intellectual activity in her list of accomplishments.

Even in the mid- to late nineteenth century it was customary for middle- and upper-class girls' physical activity to be curtailed because well-brought-up girls didn't run or even walk very much. Women in Oxford, for instance, were accustomed to using bath chairs to take them to town while the men walked beside them, and bicycling was slow to be introduced because it was deemed unladylike. Tennis became acceptable in the late nineteenth century, providing you didn't work up too much of a sweat. The sedentary work involved in embroidery, sewing and similar craft work was therefore seen as what a lady should aspire to.

While the WI has certainly never sought to limit what women do, craft work has always been an important focus. In the nineteen twenties and thirties this emphasis was a means initially of restoring knowledge of traditional village crafts, boosting the self-esteem of the members, showing to both the world at large and to the women themselves that their work had a value, that they could create beautiful objects to rank with anything men could achieve. Things were made for the women's families and friends such as baby clothes, shawls for newborns and jumpers for growing children. Skills such as rush-weaving, rag rug making and raffia work were acquired so that people's homes could be refurbished. Sewing skills such as dress-making, smocking and embroidery were also taught. Not only did people work for themselves and their families, they knitted for distressed families abroad, and in times of war they knitted for the troops. They also worked for the branch, to bolster their sense of group solidarity and to beautify their surroundings, by embroidering table covers and making banners. And of course all the work was subjected to the scrutiny of other branch members and other branches, and prizes were awarded for the best.

To ensure that standards were high and stayed that way, in 1920 the WI had established a Guild of Learners, whose aim was 'to regain the practice of home handicrafts with a view to restoring the best traditional English workmanship,' and to 'assist in bringing the best instruction in handicrafts within reach of villages'. People were interested in practical skills, even taking instruction in what had been considered men's jobs such as cobbling or tinkering, and in Elsfield, at least, new skills such as soldering. There were proficiency tests which had to be taken if someone wanted to be a demonstrator, instructor or judge.

Exhibitions of craft work were very early on the scene. In 1916 the AOS, John Nugent Harris's organisation, took a stand at the National Welfare and Economy Exhibition in Hyde Park to publicise the Women's Institute Movement. Soft toys featured rather prominently in this exhibition and a rather ugly toy rabbit called Cuthbert caught everyone's attention. In 1918 an exhibition and sale of work was organised to raise funds for the newly formed National Federation. It made a profit of £330 and was rated a huge success. Banners demonstrating the county federations' success were awarded to the ones which gained most prizes in the different categories. Following the success of this exhibition, many counties began to organise their own. In contrast, a national exhibition organised by the V&A in 1922 had no sales, no competitions and no prizes. It was purely a display of the very best work the WI could produce. Each county was limited to eighteen objects and these included banners, pictures, smocks, plain needlework, gloves and weaving.

In 1932 the National Federation organised a Handicraft Exhibition in which the Berkshire Federation exhibited an entire bedroom and its contents made by its members. And I mean everything: carpet, curtains, furniture, light shades. The *Newbury Herald* waxed lyrical about it. 'Here,' it said, 'was an exhibition where women reigned supreme. Not only did they excel at such crafts as are their own particular monopolies, but in man's sphere, too – in carpentry and wood carving, upholstery, furnishing and carpet making – there was work of a very high standard from the hands of women.' The carpet of the Berkshire house had cost less than £5 and was made with a new technique, plait stitching. The *Herald* was also impressed with the Yorkshire entry where the tiles of the fireplace were handmade while the pottery was made by the same lady from the clay in her own garden.

These exhibitions continued at regular intervals between the wars, though naturally there were none organised between 1939 and 1945. Soon after the war ended in 1946, Leamington Spa organised a 'Craftswomen at work' exhibition, which consisted of practical demonstrations of spinning and weaving, glove making, toy making, patchwork and three kinds of embroidery, as well as plain sewing.

The next national exhibition was held at the V&A in 1952, where the centrepiece was a wall hanging – 'Women's Work in Wartime' – which featured such activities as firefighting and welding. It now hangs in the Imperial War Museum. Exhibitions continued to be organised at eight- or ten-yearly intervals for the rest of the century, culminating in a 'Millennium Craft Spectacular' held at Tatton Park in Cheshire and showing 800 exhibits, selected from the 12,000 submitted. The most recent exhibition has been a travelling one organised in 2007 and entitled 'Textile Treasures of the WI', chosen from the 9,000 items belonging to the different branches of the WI and accompanied by a book of the same name.

Banners

WI banners did not spring fully formed from the imaginations of the first women who joined the organisation. Banners existed before the WI was formed, being an integral part of political life in the nineteenth century. The trade unions had very large banners made for outdoor use and often painted in oils on rubberised silk. Indeed there was a company, run by one George Tuthill in Spitalfields in the East End of London where the Huguenot silk weavers lived, whose sole source of work was the making of these splendid banners. They were expensive, but in those days, when the only way of advertising your message was to get out into the street and present it as eye-catchingly as possible, the banner was the obvious choice. Large, colourful, with a statement about the aims of the group, they provided not only the means of educating others but also of identifying themselves to others, saying, 'This is our group. This is what we represent.'

The suffragists used the same technique to good effect. Grace Hadow, the first vice-president of the WI, had been at Oxford University when the Women's Suffrage Society was founded and had walked in procession to the Albert Hall in 1908 behind their magnificent banner. The women's suffrage banners were lighter than the union ones, embroidered, stencilled or appliquéd, and created within the movement. The banners thus used women's traditional needlework skills and arrived at their designs by pooling ideas, much as WI branches still do.

Since the WI is staunchly un-party political, it would be inappropriate for their banners to have a political message, but they are often a strong statement of place and the values the WI represents. The people who have made these banners have thought long and hard before choosing how to do this. Jane Madden of Marston WI, for instance, who has recently made a banner to commemorate the ninetieth anniversary of the Marston branch, says that they needed to decide how they could represent the two communities of Marston – Old and New – and what joined the two communities together. They settled on the River Cherwell, which flows through both communities, and to tie the villages to the city of Oxford, of which they are a part, Magdalen Tower, the Radcliffe Camera and St Mary's church form the background behind the trees. The Marston banner is quite small – sixty-seven centimetres by forty-three – and beautifully sewn, with the picture appliquéd on to the background with blanket stitch. This is typical of modern banners. They are light in weight, feature exquisite embroidery and often have a frame of patchwork.

In the very early days of the WI, the V&A put on a course on banner making, tutored by Commander Kettlewell, whose wife was president of the Burford branch of the WI and who himself had an important position in the Village Clubs Association. His advice was commendably practical. He specified that designs should be bold enough to be seen from a distance and that the lettering should be clear, well spaced and readable from twenty yards away. 'Letters about three inches high should be sufficient,' he said, 'and should be of a size to be conveniently carried by an average woman in a wind. Let it be remembered the chief considerations in a banner are legibility, form, colour and material.' He went on to design the banners for Carterton and Clanfield, both in West Oxfordshire.

It is a mistake to think that every branch approached the making of a banner with confidence. For some branches it was a huge undertaking and a leap into the unknown. How did you choose a theme? How did you choose colours? How did you decide on material and how did you transfer the design on to the large piece of material? What sort of stitches did you use? Where to begin? In November 1948 Marcham WI thought long and hard about how to do it. Unsure how to begin, they first of all formed a banner subcommittee, which agreed to try and co-opt a local artist and to contact the NFWI to ask about exhibitions of banners, general advice on how to go about it and whether there were rules about colour schemes. The branch members thought it might be a good idea to portray Marcham village, so, in the words of the secretary, 'for this reason the Banner Sub-Committee would like the general meeting to submit any bits of local history known'. One member told the company how 'Abingdon Abbey is connected with some old French Abbey, and that is why the fleur de lys is to be found in Marcham'. A flower border was suggested and one member asked 'if there was any species of plant peculiar to the district'. After that they sent a couple of members of the subcommittee up to London to visit the Royal School of Needlework and the Victoria & Albert Museum. Some six months later they had 'a very charming design'. The central feature was 'a Pigeon House set in a field between two conventual [*sic*] fruit trees, with lambs in the foreground and pigeons flying overhead.' To cover the cost of the banner 'it was suggested that a Bring and Buy Stall or a Jumble Sale should be held during the year and that the General Committee should be asked if they would be willing to allot half the trading profits and tea profits for the year towards the cost'. The cost of materials was £6 18s 4d and professional advice £1 1s. It was proposed that the design poster of the banner would be framed and presented to Denman College, to be hung in the Berkshire Room.

The history of a place is often, though not invariably, stitched into a banner. Didcot's banner was initially noticeable for what it did not represent – the three cooling towers, which could be seen for miles around. These were left out, because they were thought to be ugly. Now the towers have been decommissioned and demolished, history has caught up with the town as it is presented in idealised form on the banner.

Sometimes a banner demonstrates how the village has changed over time. Stanton Harcourt has two banners; the older of the two shows the violets, known as Sutton violets, which were grown commercially and sent by rail to Covent Garden. They were picked in February, twelve to a bunch, by children, and it was very cold on the hands! Unfortunately there is no record of the date the banner was made as all records before 1960 were destroyed by an outgoing secretary, who was extremely angry at being ousted from the job. The second banner, made to replace the first, shows the arms of the family at the local manor house, the trade in violets having disappeared. Sometimes designs don't quite work out as planned. One branch president ruefully admitted that their appliqued pieces of work to represent various aspects of their particular village looked remarkably like Mickey Mouse, and it did!

In prosperous times banners have been made with the best materials available, the early ones often on silk or felt, while others have used cotton or linen. In the difficult days in the 1940s when cloth was still rationed, Edna Harris appliquéd a picture of a local medieval landowner's tomb using her mother's nightie, for want of any other suitable material. Her mother couldn't complain, as it was she who suggested her daughter make the banner.

Table Covers

Table covers are the most common kind of textile made by WI branches. Banners have traditionally been used to identify the group in the outside world, and table covers do the same in the place where people meet. They often have the name of the branch embroidered on them and sometimes they record the signatures of the members. Askham Bryan in North Yorkshire East, for instance, has the signatures of over 400 speakers and committee members between 1965 and 2006, including Mrs Dench, the mother of the actor Judi Dench, embroidered higgledy-piggledy across the face of the cloth. Saltford, Avon, had a cloth made in 1978 to celebrate the sixtieth anniversary of the founding of the branch which records every member of the group that year. The signatures here are inscribed in concentric circles, while Corfe in Somerset chose a square to record the names and dates of the presidents of the branch. Flower designs are common, perhaps because of the easy availability of transfers, and fruit was a recurrent motif in the 1930s and 1940s. The materials that were used varied. At the beginning of the movement cloths were brought from home to give a touch of warmth and friendliness to sometimes bleak village halls. These, and early examples of cloths made specifically for the branch, were often made of linen, but by the 1940s and 1950s felt became common. It was easy to handle and did not fray, which made it a good material for group work and striking designs. Its big drawback was that it was not easily washable because the colours ran, and wool embroidery, which was often used, could be distorted by the washing process.

Wall Hangings

Wall hangings are another means of decoration. Painswick in Gloucestershire has four delightful wall hangings depicting the four seasons. Designed by Miss Joan West in 1946 and stitched by thirteen members of the branch, they hang in the town hall. Wall hangings are often made to commemorate events, and Audley and Buerton in Cheshire made their wall hanging in 1984 for the NFWI 'Life and Leisure' exhibition at Olympia. It is a very colourful representation of the local community and the activities that go on there. The pale blue panels contrast well with the dark blue background, and the hanging is now housed in the church at Hankelow, a nearby village. One of the most impressive wall hangings made by WI members is the 'Women in Wartime' now housed at the Imperial War Museum in London.

The most modern wall hangings are the decorative panels in the foyer of the Diamond Light Source at Harwell in Oxfordshire. The Diamond Light Source is a very large doughnut-shaped building which houses a synchrotron. This is a machine that generates brilliant beams of light a billion times brighter than the sun. These beams can be used to explore the structure of materials and molecules. Some of the results of these explorations have been to show how the various molecules of diseases are structured, which helps in the fight to cure or ameliorate a particular condition. Some of their current research projects are to seek an understanding of how HIV and other retroviruses infect human or animal cells, to study protein structures to improve chemotherapy drugs for cancer, and to investigate tissue to improve metal hip replacement technology.

The techniques are almost impossible for any but a highly trained scientist to understand. The building is futuristic and not at all domestic in scale, so could be seen as alien and intrusive in a rural part of the country. But the centre wanted to communicate with the local population about its work in order that people clearly understood what the synchrotron could do and its positive effect on the population as a whole. Together with the Oxford Trust, a charity formed to encourage the study and understanding of science, and the Oxfordshire Federation of Women's Institutes, they decided on a project entitled *Designs for Life*, which was funded by the Wellcome Trust. The aim was to promote a better understanding of how science at Diamond Light Source could help in the fight against disease, and the method was to ask the Oxfordshire Federation of WIs to show the result of some of their work in a format the WI was good at: textiles. A leading textile artist, Anne Griffiths, herself a WI member, was engaged to lead the project and said at the time, 'One of my personal goals is to get every scientist plus as many WI members as possible to take up the stitching challenge. Just like science, stitching is for everyone.'

I had heard and read about this project and expected to see a large wall hanging in the atrium. When I entered the building there was no large wall hanging to be seen, but a collection of thirty panels, each half a metre square. Many, but not all, have been designed by Anne Griffiths and are based on the pictures of molecular structures the synchrotron produced.

All the squares are astonishingly colourful and detailed and the embroidery is extraordinarily complex. They demonstrate not only how complicated the information received from the synchrotron is, but also how much dedicated work has gone into creating these pictures. The asthma and pollen square made by Chilton WI, for instance, has orange and red ball shapes on a green background. The balls are lightly padded to give them a slight 3D effect and the orange plush velvet has been dyed so it is subtly variegated. The smaller balls that overlie the bigger orange and red ones are made of patchwork, with braid stitched over the joins in the fabric. To achieve the subtlety of colour for the braid, Judy Goodall, a member of the branch and a one-time member of a spinning and weaving group, wove it on an inkle loom, a loom used specifically for the job. The whole of the panel was sewn by hand.

One of the co-ordinators, Maureen White, remembers the day they did the dyeing. They were told to wear their oldest clothes, which was just as well as they spent a fair amount of time kneeling on the floor stirring material round in buckets of dye. There was powdered dye in large quantities, but few amenities – just one sink and a number of electric sockets. Water had to be boiled in electric kettles to provide hot water to dissolve the dyes, the loos were a very long way away and difficult to find, and they had to bring packed lunches. The different kinds of material were all white to begin with but were dyed in a spectrum of colours to give an overall unity to the different squares.

Jane Madden joined with Maureen to do a panel on osteoporosis. They decided to work from a photocopy of the deterioration of bone structure that this disease causes. Jane described the beauty of bone eaten away to a lacy network, with layer on layer of bone showing through. The base of orange cotton was covered with a bandage-like material, scrim, which was so loosely woven it could be pushed about and made full of holes. 'It was incredibly difficult material to handle because the scrim was so flimsy,' said Jane. 'When it was finished and we put all the pictures together at the Diamond Light Centre, the scientists said they could recognize what our picture represented. We felt very proud. It was very exciting to see our traditional skills used in such a modern setting.'

The Environmental Movement

Concern for and love of the countryside is often expressed not just in practical schemes such as litter picking but in the needlework produced by members. Their care and attachment to their locality is shown in banners such as Colwall's, made in 1932, with its portrayal of the Colwall apple and the Malvern hills, or Flaxley's banner in Gloucestershire, made in 1989, which shows a major building in the village flanked by the local flora and fauna, including the Blaisdon Red plum.

With their singing of 'Jerusalem', the WI had adopted the values expressed in that anthem; they loved their 'green and pleasant land' and wanted to protect it against the voracious appetites of developers and visitors who appeared not to care for the countryside around them. This love of the countryside continued and morphed during the course of the century into a concern with the environment and increasingly with global warming.

Way back in the 1930s people were expressing reservations about the development of housing in the countryside. In 1938, before the bombing that destroyed so much of the housing stock, Lady Denman had warned against wholesale building of new developments. 'We are countrywomen and our home is the countryside,' she said. 'A small development in the wrong place can destroy a whole district of many square miles.' Even Susan Buchan in Elsfield had complained about the amount of litter and wondered if manufacturers could be persuaded to make wrapping paper which rotted down quickly. In 1938 the National Federation tabled a resolution about the preservation of the countryside of outstanding natural beauty. This led in 1949 to the National Parks and Access to the Countryside Act, which set up the National Parks, of which there are now fifteen in England and Wales, ranging alphabetically from the Brecon Beacons to the Yorkshire Dales.

In 1954 Lady Brunner initiated the 'Keep Britain Tidy' campaign, based on a WI resolution. This campaign is still active today. It became an independent campaigning group in the 1960s and gained its first government grant in 1969.

Beautiful Britain happened in 1983, and featured the queen mother, the most prestigious member of the WI, planting the first of 25,000 bulbs in Hyde Park. *Home and Country* noted that the Woodland Trust had finally purchased 500 acres of woodland, thus preventing its conversion to conifers. Though not stated in the article, the Forestry Commission's policy at this time was to plant firs in large quantities as a commercial crop. The aim of that organisation has now changed and is, according to its website, to promote the sustainable management of woodland. Diversification is the name of the game now, to combat pests and disease and to prepare for climate change.

Before people were aware of climate change as an issue, 15 million trees were destroyed by the huge storm which swept through southern England in 1987. The Isle of Wight alone lost thousands of trees, glass houses had been destroyed, sheds and houses were wrecked, roads were closed and electricity and telephones were cut off. This was just the kind of situation where the network of rural branches of the WI came into its own. Forty federations responded to a survey of the havoc wrought by the hurricane, and the following year *Home and Country* reported that the replanting had begun.

In 1988 resolutions for the AGM covered such matters as the ozone layer and chlorofluorocarbons (CFCs). CFCs were used as propellants in aerosols and as a coolant in refrigerators. They were damaging the ozone layer, which protects against ultraviolet light, which in its turn causes skin cancer and cataracts. The WI were right to be concerned, but were probably rather late in expressing their concern, as the scientific community had been aware of the problem twenty years earlier, and the use of CFCs in refrigerators was banned in 1989. They were also concerned about reducing water pollution and increasing recycling. The recycling of waste paper, which had gone out of fashion in the 1970s because of a fall in the price that made it uneconomical to reprocess, had made a comeback, but it was noted that only 14 per cent of glass was currently recycled. The national executive, through the medium of *Home and Country*, stressed the need for saving energy by such methods as using the new long-life light bulbs, making sure you had a jacket on your hot water cylinder, taking a shower rather than a bath and putting aluminium foil behind radiators to improve their efficiency. They also encouraged readers to don an extra jumper in cold weather, rather than turn up the heat.

There was a flurry of activity in the 1980s at branch level that saw some WI branches succeed in their campaigns but others lose. The year 1989 saw success for Dentdale WI's five-year campaign to keep the Settle–Carlisle railway open, while in Bricket Wood in Hertfordshire a campaign to save some ancient woodland from development resulted in their council being taken to the High Court to prevent the destruction of a well-loved part of the village.

Today the NFWI is actively involved in campaigning on a variety of issues concerning the environment, in particular global warming and the need for healthy food. They do this by joining with the many other pressure groups for particular projects. In 2013, as part of the 'Stop Climate Chaos Coalition', the NFWI chairman, Ruth Bond, participated in a demonstration – 'Green is Working' – outside the treasury. Ruth said, 'WI members have been passionate about preserving and protecting the environment since the WI's inception in 1915, which has never been more important than it is now. The government needs to stop playing roulette with our green energy policy and start listening to our demands for a greener future for Britain.' The WI has helped to achieve 10 million pounds in funding for research into pollinators' health, investigating threats to the honey bee population.

In 2011 the NFWI lobbied the European Parliament to commit to introducing a mandatory country of origin label on all meat.

An example of misleading labelling was that sausages produced in this country could be labelled as 'Made in Great Britain', when in fact the meat had been sourced from abroad but the sausages made here. They followed this lobby with the Great Food Debate, a highly complex subject which included discussion of the increasing cost of food, which may lead to civil unrest, the pros and cons of genetically modified crops, ways to cut down food waste, and support for farmers so they are paid a reasonable amount of money for their produce.

The WI was a founder of the Fairtrade movement, which has had notable success with ensuring a fair price for such foodstuffs imported from abroad as coffee and bananas. Some 20 per cent of roast and ground coffee and the same proportion of bananas sold in Britain are now Fairtrade.

The WI involvement with the environmental movement has deepened over the years. It has moved from being concerned with the appearance of the countryside – picking up litter and planting bulbs – to a serious commitment to climate change, which in its turn must lead to serious lifestyle changes for all of us. Members have also done sterling work in keeping alive skills which might have disappeared but which are now making a comeback, thanks to the new groups that are springing up. The idea of market stalls bringing produce direct from growers to the local public has been taken over in some areas by farmers' markets, but let's not forget that the WI was there first.

THE CALENDAR GIRLS AND BEYOND

In the second half of the twentieth century, the WI had something of a problem with the way it was viewed by the general public. From the beginning of the organisation and up to and during the Second World War, members were thought of and thought of themselves as the bedrock of British society. They were the guardians of tradition, with, before the Second World War, access to government and substantial influence on government policy. If politicians wanted to know – and sometimes if they didn't – what the view of the sensible middle-of-the-road woman was, they went to the WI. During the war, this bedrock kept things together. They welcomed evacuees – well, at least until they found how very different city children were from their own well-brought-up, obedient and above all clean children. They made jam by the bucketful and thereby kept the shelves of the country's grocery shops stacked with produce. They grew vegetables and sold them on market stalls. They expressed their creativity in beautiful handcrafted garments and items for the home, and they showed their devotion to their particular bit of England or Wales in the banners they made, which often showed the essence of their countryside – the church, the local buildings, the flowers, the crops. They were rooted in the British countryside and that is how the world saw them. So far so good.

After the war, times and the country changed. The government was busy implementing a quiet revolution and bringing to fruition a large part of what the WI had campaigned for before the war: clean water, sanitation, electricity and contact with the outside world in the way of telephones in rural villages, free grammar school education for boys and girls, grants for university education for those who wanted it and could make use of it, and universal health care in the form of the National Health Service. There was no longer such a clear mandate for the WI. The Americanisation of the country, which gathered pace over the decades following the war, made Britain look old-fashioned and a poor relation, so anyone who supported the values of the WI was similarly old fashioned. With the advent of the new feminists in the 1970s and 1980s domesticity went out of the window. Many women were trying to be superwomen doing everything: running a home, taking responsibility for the children, holding down a job. Books were published on how to do it, one recommendation being to get rid of the blankets and buy duvets for the beds. One quick flick and the bed is made. No more washing blankets in spring. Send the duvet to the cleaners and pay for it with the money you've earned in your job.

By 1970 the president of the WI, Miss Sylvia Grey, was writing in *Home and Country* that 'the Press are beginning to report our activities more accurately, or do I mean more kindly? We realise we are a sitting target for "knocking", after all we wear hats, we sing Jerusalem and we make jam.' The WI obviously had a problem with the press and how the press represented them. Again in 1989, Penny Kitchen, the editor of *Home and Country*, complained that the visit of President Bush had pushed news of the AGM off the front pages, and all the papers, not just the tabloids, included a picture of women picnicking on the grass with none of them even mentioning the resolutions, which included the topics of hazardous waste and deforestation. If 6,000 men had assembled to discuss such things, it would have been news, she said. As it was, 'nice as the singing of "Jerusalem" is and the picnic, national and global issues should take prominence', she wrote. She was so incensed that she wrote to the editor of her favourite paper to complain, but it was not published.

Around the turn of the century there were two events which presented a different picture of the WI and which did make the front pages of the newspapers. One was the humiliation of Tony Blair, who was barracked at the AGM. The press's indifference to what 6,000 women were doing was overcome by their delight that the Prime Minister had been publicly humiliated. According to Jane Robinson's account of the incident in her book *A Force to be Reckoned with*, the Prime Minister's office had asked if he could speak at the AGM some time the previous year, but there had been no follow-up from his office and the national executive assumed that he would not be coming. When they were informed that he would be there, they had to shuffle round the speakers to make space for him and he was warned not to be late and not to give a party-political speech, as the WI is a non-party-political organisation. So he was only twenty minutes late and as a committed politician, probably didn't know where statesman finished and party politician began. He was sometimes inaudible, as he'd asked for an autocue, which the WI refused to supply on the grounds of expense, so he had to turn away from the microphone to consult his notes. All in all it was not a successful performance. In the event, while it proved something of a disaster for Tony Blair, it at least broke down, even if only momentarily, the press's reluctance to feature the WI.

The other event which interested the press was the calendar made by the women of Rylstone and District WI, North Yorkshire, who turned personal tragedy into a collective triumph. These women made such an impact on public awareness that I hardly need to explain what they did. But just in case you haven't heard, they decided to produce a calendar with twelve of their members posing in the nude to raise money, initially for a new sofa in the hospital waiting room where the husband of one of the members was being treated for leukaemia. The sale of the calendar raised so much money that they were able to fund a unit at the University of Leeds for research into the causes and possible cures for leukaemia. This story was a gift to the film industry, a feel-good story which contrasted the perceived image of the WI, a staid and elderly organisation, with the reality. The film *Calendar Girls* brought the story to a worldwide audience.

Ironically the film has a heroine, played by Helen Mirren, who rejects the domesticity celebrated by the WI, and wins a cake competition with a bought cake from Marks and Spencer. (This could never actually happen. Bought cakes, good as they may be, are instantly recognisable as such because they taste different from fresh homemade cake, though some people may prefer the taste.) Mirren addresses the AGM and announces to the assembled throng that 'I 'ate plum jam.'(Meaning 'I hate', not 'I consumed'.) While thus forcefully rejecting the idea of domesticity that may have been the public perception of the organisation, the film equally forcefully emphasises the WI ethos of help and friendship among women and powerfully asserts the beauty of the human body at any age, thereby rejecting the modern fixation with youth and youthful image.

The Calendar Girls, both the real ones and the film version, overturned the idea of the WI as an old-fashioned collection of elderly ladies who made jam and sang 'Jerusalem'. Here was a group of brave and imaginative women who raised thousands of pounds for their chosen charity, who brought fame to their little bit of Yorkshire, and who caught the imagination of the film industry. This was what women could do when they got together and turned their collective energies to something worthwhile and daring. The film showed a group of women with familiar faces – and now bodies! – from television and film acting in contravention of the norms of their village because they needed to do something they thought important. The film actually misrepresented the NFWI's role in the whole adventure, because the National Federation was whole-heartedly behind the idea.

The film, though, because of its likeable characters and its demonstration of a congenial group of people acting together to help in the fight against cancer, has raised the profile of the WI. Since then, there has been a renewed interest in the organisation and an upsurge in the formation of new branches. These are made up of predominantly young women, and though they say they welcome all ages, and I'm sure they do, their activities appeal to the chronologically young and the young at heart. Their titles, full of humour and media references, reflect this new stance: the Shoreditch Sisters in London, Tea and Tarts in Huddersfield, Buns and Roses in Leeds, Disparate Housewives in Hampshire, Tea Birds and Polly Dollies in Oxfordshire. These are not exclusively rural branches. They often use town or city-centre premises, and the subjects of their meetings reflect their youth: belly dancing, fencing, a night of Northern soul dancing to Motown music. But the heart of the WI ethos is observed; these are 'local women getting together to learn new skills, meet like-minded friends, and of course occasionally making jam', as the Tea and Tarts web site has it. The skills they learn – welding, silk painting, bicycle maintenance, Caribbean cooking, and in some cases their overt sexuality – would have surprised the early members of the WI, but the likes of Grace Hadow and Trudie Denman would have applauded these vigorous and feisty new groups.

And what of the WI today? The WI is the largest women's organisation in Britain, with 205,000 members. The movement is on the increase. It has recently acquired 112 new branches and 21,000 new members. This could easily mean that in such a large organisation people could lose touch with the centre and feel a lack of connection to other groups, but this is not the case. People keep in touch with other branches via the county organisation magazine and the national magazine, once called *Home and Country*, now *WI Life*. Each branch is linked to a number of other branches in its vicinity and often meets with them on a regular basis. The WI is also linked to women's organisations in other countries via the Associated Country Women of the World, founded in 1933 by Madge Watt.

The ideas which concerned the WI when it first began – breaking down the isolation of women in outlying areas, issues around women's education and the welfare of mothers and children in rural villages – have largely been addressed in one way or another, but as the Oxfordshire Federation chairman says, the organisation still 'works hard to address current issues which concern women, the communities we live in, our families and our future. We are a respected organisation as reflected by the increasing number of agencies which seek our help and support and we have the lobbying power to influence government.'

The WI has representatives on the executives of an astonishing number of pressure groups focusing on a variety of interests: violence against women, the environment, health and justice, the Gender and Development Network, the Trade Justice movement, and the British Nutrition Foundation. The WI is also represented on what one might think of as more traditional territory, such as the National Trust and the National Institute for Clinical Excellence (NICE). At the present time, support for British agriculture, the importation of foodstuffs and small abattoirs are just some of the issues on the campaigning agenda. Underlining the WI's interest in local history, and having made so much of it themselves, 2012 was the year of the Archive, when every branch was expected to organise their copies of old minutes, scrap books and mementoes. Many a branch secretary has groaned at the work this important task has entailed, but has gone about it with a will, however reluctant. The year 2013 was the year of the Great Food Debate, which considered farming methods, food waste, genetically modified crops, water supply, sustainability, home-grown foods, pricing and climate change. No small undertaking!

The county organisation is an important part of the structure of the National Federation. One of the schemes it has devised to stimulate interest in learning is to run a quiz night where teams from the various branches compete for a cup. They are light-hearted affairs; one team leader, Sue Phipps, rallied her troops with the reassurance that everyone knows something. An observation borne out when eighty-six-year-old Marjorie, who had walked into the venue with her white stick, when asked what sport the term 'ippon' was used in, promptly replied correctly, 'Judo.' Her grandson was keen on judo. 'We never win,' says Sue, 'but it's fun to take part.' Her team scored a respectable forty-seven out of ninety, only six less than the winning team, and went home relieved that they wouldn't have to proceed to a more difficult set of questions. The Sassy Girls from Stroud Green in Middlesex had better luck, or knowledge, in their federation competition as they tackled questions such as the main ingredient of baba ganoush (aubergine) and how many players in a curling team (four), winning their heat to go forward to the regional and perhaps the national finals.

Each county organisation is allotted a three-day period at Denman College, where members can study a range of topics. When Cumbria county federation visited Denman in September 2013 they studied dressing with style, posh picnics and fabulous fascinators, and they went on a walk from Larkrise to Candleford, quite a distance, with a talk on Flora Thompson thrown in for good measure. However, Denman College has, and has had for some time, a funding problem. It is an expensive place to maintain, so to cover costs every day of the year has to be filled with people eager to sample what is on offer. This is a difficult job. And the price of the courses is not cheap. A two-day course on bead weaving and bead embroidery, for instance, costs £247 plus £15 for materials. This is not an unreasonable price to pay, but is a large amount for someone who does not have a regular and fairly substantial income. There is also the ever-escalating cost of getting there.

Every year each county federation holds an AGM. I attended the Oxfordshire Federation of Women's Institutes' Annual Council meeting in March 2013 in Oxford Town Hall. It was a bitterly cold day but the welcome was warm. The officers sat on the stage behind a table draped in the splendidly embroidered dark blue cloth of the Oxfordshire Federation, the initials OFWI picked out in bold white letters and surrounded by beautifully embroidered white flowers, a stunning example of the skills of the federation. Everyone rose to their feet and sang 'Jerusalem', a clichéd yet still moving experience, not because it speaks of bows of burning gold or arrows of desire but mainly because it speaks of 'our green and pleasant land'.

Then the business of the day began. Spotted among the audience in the lunch break and noticeable because of their youth and the fact that they were eating sushi rather than cheese sandwiches were two young women, Charlotte and Cally, who are part of the new group the Tea Birds. The group was only formed in February, so they were inexperienced in being part of the WI. They helped form the group because they wanted to make new friends. 'I work for the police so there's a lot of shift work,' said Charlotte, 'and my life seemed to be just work and thinking about work. A lot of the friends I had at school have moved away and I wanted to start something new. I'd like to learn some of the traditional crafts like knitting and crochet. We weren't taught things like that at school.' Cally confirmed what Charlotte had to say. She too wanted to learn new skills.

The thing about a group is that you can try things out without having the embarrassment of admitting what you don't know, or spending a lot of money on trying to teach yourself something and failing. I hope we'll do something about car maintenance. In a group you can try things out. For instance, we've had a go at quilling.

[Quilling is an art form using strips of paper rolled and glued to make patterns.] I wasn't much good at it but it was fun to try, and we had a lot of laughs.

'We're having a "speed-dating" session next meeting,' says Charlotte. 'Of course, we're not looking for a partner, but we can use the same technique to meet people we don't know and find out about their lives. I think it's a brilliant way of getting to know other people in the group. We've got a mixture of ages. One woman brought her new baby to the meeting the other night.'

Tea Birds was started by Jo Christie. When asked why it had occurred to her to start a new branch, she said, 'I have always been interested in the kind of activities the WI do and am interested in what it has achieved so I was drawn to it.' She had joined various groups in the past and found people she liked and a skill she enjoyed when she joined a sewing group, but this only gave one outlet to her creativity. She has a great many interests – she keeps chickens and has dogs and likes vintage clothes and felt that groups catering only for one particular aspect of life, especially if it concerned appearance, which many women's groups do, would not fulfil any need she had for friendship or to increase her skills. She looked on the Internet and found the Buns and Roses website of the Leeds-based group. 'I thought something like that would be just what we wanted,' said Jo. She uses social networks a lot so started a Facebook discussion group about it. She received over eighty responses, and when she organised a meeting twenty-five people turned up. By that time, though, she had organised a Facebook page for the group. Using this they had already chosen a name and had a logo, and a website soon followed. 'You can get going very quickly,' said Jo, and it's easy to keep in touch with people and remind them of what's happening. It's a long time between meetings so I put reminders up about the meeting, and anything useful I think people might be interested in. For instance, I've just put a link up to knitting patterns. It's important to keep up a presence. I read up about the Women's Institute – they have a very good website – so I knew what the WI stood for, and how to set up a branch and I knew about Denman College. We have a lot of skilled, confident women now and we can use their skills. Cally, for instance, is a marketing manager so she's done our website and our treasurer is a trained accountant. We have spin off groups – knitting and crochet, cycling, walking and rambling.

When asked about politics, she says that at the moment that hasn't surfaced as an interest but with the resolutions taken up by the WI there is no reason why they shouldn't develop that side of things. 'I think it's very sad that girls are encouraged to put such a lot of stress on their appearance,' she says thoughtfully. 'It would be nice to be able to provide some sort of alternative role model which is more fulfilling, just as the Federation Annual Meeting does for us,' she adds.

The liveliest of the branches and county federations provide social contact and information on a variety of subjects, as diverse as 'Life under the veil', 'Journey to the North Pole, 'History of English furniture' and 'Life of a Lady Bailiff'. Skittles, Scrabble and quiz nights are also part of the scene, as are fundraising events such as coffee mornings. Every branch offers a different experience because of their autonomy and the different interests and expertise of members.

But it would be dishonest to pretend that everything in the

garden is rosy. There are moribund branches that have not attracted new members. One of the perennial problems is making sure there is a president. According to the constitution, each branch must have a president who will take responsibility for the group, even if they don't do a huge amount of work. Elsfield WI foundered in 1963 for precisely that reason. Marston has had a few problems in spite of their president Theresa Bentley's repeated efforts to find a successor. Perhaps the problem lies partly in the title 'president', with its connotations of unlimited power (think President Obama). Stanion WI in Northamptonshire, however, does not have that problem. The president, Rachel MacAllister, the youngest president in the county, set up the group in a village where there are very few community amenities, and the group offers pole-dancing lessons as one of its activities. Meanwhile, Hayden WI in Hampshire, with an older demographic, has started a ukulele band, tutored by the fourteen-year-old grandson of one of the members.

Out of this mixture of events and interests comes occasionally a matter that grabs the attention of the whole country. Such was the case with Jean Johnson and Shirley Landels, of the Hampshire Federation. In 2007, appalled by the murder of several prostitutes in Suffolk, Hampshire county federation tabled a motion at the autumn council meeting that 'HCFWI urges local authorities to provide safe working spaces for the operation of brothels'. They felt there was a need 'to discuss women's issues, such as prostitution, in an informed, rational, supportive and compassionate way'. Channel Four, the television channel, their interest perhaps piqued by this conjunction of extreme respectability as represented by the WI and its opposite, prostitution, sent Jean, the proposer of the motion, and Shirley, the seconder, on a fact-finding mission to America, Amsterdam and New Zealand. Since the programme was aired, Jean has addressed and had discussions with a number of concerned people – MPs and peers, the Royal College of Nursing and the English Collective of Prostitutes. She has also spoken to student bodies in various universities, including Oxford, Manchester and Bristol.

Sometimes the anger of the branch focuses on something near home. When Eva-Marie Allen was out walking her dog in Charlwood, Surrey, she was attacked by a man, who hit her on the head with a stone. The branch decided to do something about it. They asked a Taekwondo expert to teach them how to defend themselves, which he did in four sessions. Eva-Marie advanced to such a level of expertise that she was able to break a brick with one blow of her hand. The Taekwondo techniques gave the whole group a sense of belief in their ability to defend themselves, and restored Eva-Marie's confidence, which of course had been severely dented when she was attacked. The course turned a very negative experience into a positive event for the women of the group.

The WI has always been aware, it seems to me, of women outside what would be considered their normal ambit. In 1925 the secretary of Headington Quarry WI wrote that following a discussion on the Poor Law, Mrs Jones reported that there were several women in the Headington Workhouse who would be grateful for visitors. It was suggested to the members that, if permission could be obtained, the Quarry institute would arrange to visit regularly at the workhouse. And three years later they arranged to borrow a spinal carriage so members could take one of the workhouse residents, Lilly Hedges, out for a few hours. In the 1970s there were several branches formed in long-stay hospitals, among them St James Hospital Portsmouth, which catered for people with mental disabilities. This spirit of caring for those less fortunate than themselves has been carried forward in a striking way at Bronzefield in Surrey and is involving women who are usually thought to be outside society – women in prison. The resettlement team leader at Her Majesty's Prison, Bronzefield, along with two WI advisers from the Surrey federation, have established a branch of the WI in the prison. It was established in 2011 and resulted from a Care not Custody campaign, which aimed to raise awareness of the importance of resettlement of prisoners. Bronzefield WI has about forty members and the women are passionate about their membership within a larger organisation. One of the organisers says, 'The WI provides an opportunity to co-operate and to share a positive experience.' The hope is that when the women leave custody, they will be able to form links more easily with their community through their local WI.

And now, as an example of good practice, let us consider Ottery St Mary. This is a re-formed group that was started again in 2005 by the WI adviser for the area. Ottery St Mary is a small town twelve miles from Exeter, with a very large church rivalling Exeter Cathedral in splendour, and home to a bizarre ritual that takes place on 5 November. Instead of the usual bonfire, seventeen barrels soaked in tar are lined up in front of the town's four pubs and young men, women and children carry the burning tar barrels in a race through the town. Only people born in Ottery or long-standing residents may take part, but the event attracts large numbers of people to watch. You might think that the inhabitants of a town where such an event takes place will have an eccentric or sadistic streak in them, but this is very far from the case if the WI is anything to go by. Ottery St Mary Women's Institute is a socially aware, energetic and generous group of women who have made their presence felt in the town. They have thirty-one members, ranging in age from thirty-two to eighty-four, with the majority in their forties and fifties. They regularly get twenty-five members to their meetings, though this drops in the summer to about twenty as several members go abroad for several weeks. The secretary, Sue McCarthy, keeps in touch with these people by email, keeping them informed of what is happening in the branch.

Of course, they have the usual WI activities. They have a stall at the community market, where they sell refreshments. The WI runs a cake stall but before they start selling the cakes, they take a tea trolley round and give a free drink to any stallholder who wants one. They sell bacon butties where the bacon is bought from a local butcher and the baps made by a local baker. These sell for £2 and have been very popular. They sell a slice of cake and a drink for £1 and make most of their income from this.

They have a good website and have improved their IT skills by employing a local man to teach them. They have had trips to the local courts to see how they work, to Sainsbury's before it opened to see how it is organised, and to the Great Hall at Exeter University to hear the Bournemouth Symphony Orchestra in the New Year Gala Concert. They have talks from interesting speakers and link the monthly competition to this. They have a crafty afternoon which occurs once a month and which is now involved in making bags out of scrap material – they sell these for £1 – and they have a monthly raffle. They have a flower competition. Every person brings a single flower grown in her own garden in a small vase. Everyone attending the meeting puts a silver coin by the flower she likes best, and the one with the most coins gets the most points, which are totted up at the end of the year and a trophy is awarded. The money – about £60 a year – goes into the 'Money for Friendship' pot. This supports the work of the ACWW, the organisation begun by Madge Watt, the Association of Country Women Worldwide.

And this is where the group moves beyond the ordinary to the extraordinary. They have in their group a woman, Anitra, who has worked in Pakistan with women who have suffered Female Genital Mutilation (FGM). While this is a practice often associated with African countries, there are 3,000 women at risk in Britain alone, so the matter is of relevance even in the UK. Ottery WI became aware of the problem through Anitra and via newspaper accounts, and drafted a resolution to submit to the National Federation. It was rejected by them because it was considered too closely linked to Violence Against Women, so the group decided to lobby the ACWW, to get the resolution adopted by them. It was important to have the idea couched in the right language, and for this they were guided by Anne-Marie Wilson, who had been to the town to talk on the subject. They lobbied for eighteen months and finally got their resolution adopted – one of only fourteen. This was a huge honour, and also, I think a tribute to their determination and commitment. The resolution: 'Be it resolved that ACWW calls on all people worldwide to stop the practice of Female Genital Mutilation, Female Circumcision and Cutting which endangers the health and life of young girls.' The resolution was seconded by the president of the Eire CWA. Ottery then had the task of raising the money to send Anitra to Chennai (once known as Madras) in India to present their argument. The branch secretary wrote to several airlines asking for help with the airfare, and Emirates offered a ticket at cost price. She also wrote to thirty-two branches, and was very encouraged by the response. The branch held a quiz and cream tea event attended by eighty-five people, which raised a substantial amount of money towards the trip. On 1 October the triumphant email came through: Anitra had successfully presented the proposal and it had been accepted unanimously.

It seems to me that this branch is a shining example to others. They provide support for their members, they have fun, they communicate with the outside world, and they have the imagination to empathise with women in other countries who do not enjoy the advantages that many women in Britain have. They bridge the gap between old and young and make good use of the energies of women who in their fifties and sixties might in the past have been considered old, but who are now in the prime of life. The founders of the WI, the likes of Lady Denman and Grace Hadow, would have been proud of Ottery St Mary. It represents the true spirit of the WI – the struggle to improve the lives of women – and shows that the original impetus for the movement is not dead or deflected from its purpose in spite of the different times we live in.

You won't find many revolutionaries in the ranks of the WI but you will find a great many people who believe that the slow sure way of the tortoise to further the cause of feminism wins in the end over the feverish bursts of activity from the hares of this world. In spite of the lack of focus at times, particularly in the 1980s and 1990s, I think it is fair to say that the great strength of the WI is that it is there for the long run. In battles to save the environment they were in at the beginning. They began the battles for decent rural housing, proper sewerage systems and electricity for rural communities, and kept these going for forty years. In spite of the indifference of the press and the lack of respect for women, which is still all too prevalent, they didn't give up. On 31 October 2013, commenting on the phenomenon of hundreds of women queuing to join a new branch of the WI at Bromley Heath in Bristol in 2013, *Guardian* leader writer Anne Perkins wrote,

> It [the WI] kept on trucking through the bad times when what happened at home didn't matter because it was all about being out there, consuming, not creating, succeeding on your own. Now its core value, that it's not about who you are, but what you can do, feels exactly right. Just like its appeal to community, to knowing your neighbours and having a good time together.

Or as Jo Christie puts it, 'It's really nice to feel part of a body of women of all ages who have contributed so much to improving life for women. We want to carry that on.'

BIBLIOGRAPHY

Andrews, Maggie. *The Acceptable Face of Feminism*. (London: Lawrence and Wishart, 1997.)

Bartley, Pamela. *The Changing Role of Women 1815–1914*. (London: Hodder and Stoughton, 1996.)

Bradley, K. *Faith, Perseverance and Patience: The History of the Oxford Suffrage and Anti-Suffrage Movements 1870–1930*. Unpublished PhD thesis. (Oxford: Oxford Brookes University, 1997.)

Brittain, Vera. *The Women at Oxford. A Fragment of History*. (London: Harrap, 1960.)

Buchan, William. *The Rags of Time*. (Southampton: Ashford, Buchan and Enright, 1990.)

Caine, Barbara. *Victorian Feminists*. (Oxford: Oxford University Press, 1992.)

Chadwick, Whitney. *Women, Art and Society*. (London: Thames and Hudson, 1990.)

Collins, Wilkie. *The Moonstone*. (Oxford: Oxford World Classics, first published 1868.)

Connell, Linda (ed.). *Textile Treasures of the WI*. (Southampton: The National Needlework Archive, 2007.)

Crawford, Elizabeth. *The Women's Suffrage Movement: A Reference Guide. 1866–1928*. (London: UCL Press, 1999.)

Delafield, E. M. *The Provincial Lady*. (London: Macmillan and Co., 1947.)

Deneke, Helena. *Grace Hadow*. (London: Oxford University Press, 1946.)

Deneke, Helena. *What Elsfield Remembers*. Unpublished account of the war years 1939–1945. (Oxford History Centre.)

Dibble, Jeremy. *C. Hubert H. Parry. His Life and Music.* (Oxford: Oxford University Press, 1992.)

Dudgeon, Piers (ed.). *Village Voices.* (London: Pilot Productions Ltd., 1989.)

Elliott, Dorice Williams. *The Angel out of the House. Philanthropy and Gender in Nineteenth Century England.* (Charlottesville and London: University Press of Virginia, 2002.)

Evans, Mary (ed.). *The Woman Question: Readings on the Subordination of Women.* (Oxford: Fontana, 1982.)

Gregory, Philippa, David Baldwin and Michael Jones. *The Women of the Cousins' War.* (London: Simon and Schuster, 2011.)

Hall, Lesley A. *Sex, Gender and Social Change in Britain since 1880.* (Basingstoke: Palgrave Macmillan, 2013.)

Horn, Pamela. *The Rise and Fall of the Victorian Servant.* (Stroud: Sutton Publishing, 1990.)

Horn, Pamela. *Life as a Victorian Lady.* (Stroud: Sutton Publishing, 2007.)

Huxley, Gervas. *Lady Denman.* (Worcester and London: Chatto and Windus, 1961.)

Inglis, Ruth. *The Children's War, Evacuation 1939–1945* (London: William Collins, 1989.)

Kaye, Barbara. *Live and Learn. The Story of Denman College 1948–1969.* (London: NFWI, 1970.)

Kelly, Stephen F. *You've Never Had it so Good!* (Stroud: The History Press, 2012.)

Lewis, Jane. *Women in Britain since 1945.* (Oxford: Blackwell, 1992.)

Lodge, Eleanor C. *Terms and Vacations.* (London: Oxford University Press, 1938.)

McCall, Cicely. *Women's Institutes.* (London: William Collins, 1943.)

McCall, Cicely. *Our Villages.* (London: NFWI, 1956.)

McSmith, Andy. *No Such Thing as Society.* (London: Constable, 2011.)

Parker, Rozsika. *The Subversive Stitch.* (London: I. B. Taurus, 1984.)

Purvis, June. (ed.) *Women's History. Britain 1850–1945.* (London: UCL Press, 1995.)

Robinson, Jane. *A Force to be Reckoned With. A History of the Women's Institute.* (London: Virago, 2011.)

Stamper, Anne. *Rooms off the Corridor.* (London: WI Books, 1998.)

Stewart, Sheila. *Lifting the Latch. A Life on the Land.* (Charlbury: Day Books, 2000.)

Tweedsmuir, Susan. *A Winter Bouquet.* (London: Gerald Duckworth and Co., 1954.)

Wilson, A. N. *Our Times. The Age of Elizabeth.* (London: Hutchinson, 2008.)

Winterson, Jeanette. *Why be Happy When You Could be Normal?* (London: Vintage Books, 2012.)

Wood, Victoria. *The Victoria Wood Christmas Show.* BBC, 2000.

Periodicals

WI Life. The National Magazine of the WI. Issue 50, 5 March 2013.

WI Life. The National Magazine of the WI. Issue 51, April 2013.

Websites

www.en.Wikipedia.org

Oxford Dictionary of National Biography. www.oxforddnb.com

www.OtteryStMaryWI.org.uk

www.bunsandroses.co.uk

www.tea-birdswi.co.uk

Public Record Offices and Libraries

Berkshire County Records Office, Reading

D/EX 1925.20/3/2/1-8

D/EX 1925.30/4/1/1/1-43 Photograph; Newbury market produce stall.

D/EX 1925.20/3/2/1-8 Report of delegate to National AGM 1939.

Hampshire County Record, Winchester
45M90/3 Autobiography of Phyllis M Wickham. *Fifty Years of WI: The Inside Story in Two Counties.*
96M96/84 Portsmouth St James Hospital 1975–1986

Oxfordshire History Centre
03/1/1/C1/13 Correspondence about setting up fruit preservation centres.
03/2/44/A1 Institute Committee Minutes 1920–1963.

The Women's Library, London School of Economics
Home and Country 1945–2000.
5/FWI/B/2/2/2/018 photograph.
5/FWI/B/2/2/2/022 photograph.
5/FWI/2/2/2/026 photograph.
5FWI/b/2/2/28/045 photograph.
5/FWI/E/2/01/Paper no. A23. Survey of work of voluntary organisations in provision of adult education.
5/FWI/E1/2/79 Denman Appeal Fund 1988; Scene 80.
5/FWI/E/2/01/1 Miscellaneous Documents, Letters and memoranda, 1940s – 1990s.
5/FWI/10/1/2/4 PA General 1940–1978.

ACKNOWLEDGEMENTS

I'm very grateful for all the help and support I've received from both friends and professionals in various fields – the staff at the Oxford History Centre, the Women's Library, especially Sonia Gomez and Catherine McIntyre, Berkshire Public Records Office, especially Natalie Bennet, and Hampshire Public Records Office – for their expertise, unfailing courtesy and patience. Thanks to Lesley Sexton at the John Buchan Museum for the photograph of Lady Tweedsmuir and a special thank you to Oliver Mahoney of Lady Margaret Hall for services over and above the call of duty! The *Oxford Times* for their photograph of Denman College, the Mary Evans Picture Library, and Nicola Gale and Christian Duck, my editors, for their words of wisdom.

Branches of the WI: Ottery St Mary, Headington Quarry, Thame, Marcham, Chilton, the Tea Birds, Maureen White of Wolvercote and in particular Theresa Bentley, Sue Phipps and Jane Madden of Marston WI.

Margaret Strother and Roz Tallett for observations and comments, Sally Despenser for reading and amending, John Lockwood for his ability to see a way round obstacles, Cherry Mosteshar, Sarah Shaw, Sue Hine and Cassandra Wall for their ideas and encouragement.

Lucy, for her careful reading and appraisal, Chris and Ed for IT support, Stuart for being prepared to argue a point, for chauffeuring, innumerable cups of tea and infinite patience.

INDEX

ABOUT THE AUTHOR

Mavis Curtis spent her career in primary teaching and social work and is now retired. She has a PhD from the University of Sheffield and has contributed to numerous books, journals and magazines, including *The Lore of the Playground* (Random House), a social history of children's games. During research on the WI in 2012 for the *Oxford Times*, she was overwhelmed by the friendliness of the people she met, and she is now a very enthusiastic member of the institute. She lives in Oxfordshire.